healthier

food facts **nutrition** exercise **you**

The second book in the Can Cook, Will Cook series

Edited by Robbie Davison
Contributions by Tony Evans, Clare Fox,
Rachel Long, Fiona Shaw and Helen Turner

healthier

Edited by Robbie Davison
Contributions by Tony Evans, Clare Fox, Rachel Long, Fiona Shaw and Helen Turner
Photography by Alexandra Wolkowicz
Graphic design by Mike Carney / Mike's Studio
Serotonin and endorphins sections written by Dr. Victoria Kearns
Printed and bound in Italy by Graphicom

ISBN: 978-0-9556547-4-9

First published in May 2008 by Pepper Books, an imprint of Capsica Ltd.
83 Ampthill Road, Liverpool L17 9QN

email: healthier@capsica.net
www.loveliverpoolbooks.com

Five Children and Families Trust
Conleach Road, Speke, Liverpool L24 0TW
www.cancookwillcook.org.uk
Charity no. 1112796

Proceeds from the sale of this book will go towards
developing services for children and families.

introduction

This drive to get everyone to take on a healthy lifestyle is a bit confusing. Just what is healthy? How do you know when you've got there? And who is that healthy person we should all aspire to?

If we listen to everything that we're being told, healthy means cutting out everything that we like, never drinking alcohol, exercising for hours and – in short – radically changing our lives. For most of us, healthy is just a bit too hard.

That's why we're talking about getting 'healthier'. *Healthier* has something for us all, is something real, and can be achieved and enjoyed.

Healthier is the second book in the Can Cook series. Our first, *Can Cook Will Cook: Everyday Cooking for Everyday People*, was a great success, prompted by our passion to introduce exciting recipes and cooking into people's homes.

Healthier is about building on that success and taking our passion further. This time around, we dip into the real and sometimes dark world of takeaways and provide the proof that regularly eating takeaway food leads you down a really unhealthy path. Then we introduce you to some tricks of the trade from the worlds of nutrition and exercise.

It's not about preaching, it's about providing you with the information to make choices about you and your health. In the middle section of the book we want to steer you towards cooking at home. You'll find over 50 mouth-watering recipes in *Healthier*, because we love to cook and we want everyone to feel the same way.

Mealtimes are the most important part of the day for us, and we want to get you into the kitchen, cooking and then sitting down with your family and friends to enjoy the food and the time together. Most of the recipes reflect the summer months; light, crisp and full of colour. Others are variations on those takeaway favourites, proving that, without much effort, you can have all the taste at a lower cost, and much 'healthier' too. Enjoy them.

contents

recipes

chapter 1

facts

Facts are always a good place to start a book, particularly if they've been well researched and provide us with an insight we didn't have before. Takeaway food usually tastes great and is there for us when we finish work, when the kids finish school, after a night out – all the times we want a quick food fix and are feeling a bit lazy. So, with the intention of trying to get you to think twice before buying your next takeaway, let's introduce you to some shocking facts.

the horrible truth

Nowadays, the majority of food that you buy from supermarkets contains the nutritional information to help you choose. And many supermarkets have introduced front-of-pack indicators highlighting the amount of salt, fat and calories, so you can see at a glance what the food contains and you're able to make an informed choice. Unfortunately, it's not the case in many takeaways or restaurants and the majority of us are unaware of what we're eating.

To address this, Liverpool City Council Trading Standards has developed research called 'Eatright Liverpool' which uncovered the nutritional content of takeaway food across Liverpool. They bought 300 meals from most takeaway establishments across the city and tested them for salt, fat and calories. The results were startling – so much so they added the colour black to the existing Traffic Light Labelling Scheme, to enable us all to pick out the meals we should avoid.

The graphic on the opposite page shows the 'best of the worst' – they're takeaway meals we're all familiar with, love to eat and that always tempt us back for more.

These results are taken from Liverpool, but takeaways are pretty much the same everywhere. Until things change, takeaways will remain unhealthy. We've provided some healthier recipes for your favourites on pages 94 – 97. Over the page, vital statistics shows you a healthy level of fat, salt, sugar and calories.

over **120%**	of your recommended daily amount
upto **75%–120%**	of your recommended daily amount
upto **35%–74.9%**	of your recommended daily amount
upto **35%**	of your recommended daily amount

The black boxes show the takeaways that had over 120% of your recommended daily amounts in one portion.

The Chinese meal, beef green pepper and black bean sauce with fried rice was found to contain nearly five times the daily recommended amount of salt for an adult

margherita pizza

Fat (g) per meal	**107.3**
Salt (g) per meal	**13.0**
Calories per meal	**2330**

seafood pizza

Fat (g) per meal	**149.5**
Salt (g) per meal	**11.7**
Calories per meal	**3203**

pepperoni pizza

Fat (g) per meal	**160.8**
Salt (g) per meal	**12.8**
Calories per meal	**3320**

donner kebab and chips

Fat (g) per meal	**146.2**
Salt (g) per meal	**10.1**
Calories per meal	**2934**

chicken kebab

Fat (g) per meal	**53.8**
Salt (g) per meal	**11.7**
Calories per meal	**1210**

shish kebab

Fat (g) per meal	**18.8**
Salt (g) per meal	**9.3**
Calories per meal	**643**

beef green pepper and black bean sauce with fried rice

Fat (g) per meal	**48.0**
Salt (g) per meal	**27.6**
Calories per meal	**1382**

prawn chow mein

Fat (g) per meal	**18.3**
Salt (g) per meal	**21.8**
Calories per meal	**825**

sweet and sour chicken and chips

Fat (g) per meal	**113.2**
Salt (g) per meal	**4.9**
Calories per meal	**2468**

lamb bhuna and chips

Fat (g) per meal	**129.9**
Salt (g) per meal	**6.8**
Calories per meal	**1867**

king prawn rogan josh and pilau rice

Fat (g) per meal	**57.5**
Salt (g) per meal	**9.2**
Calories per meal	**1312**

chicken tikka massalla and keema rice

Fat (g) per meal	**104.3**
Salt (g) per meal	**12.5**
Calories per meal	**1913**

fish and chips

Fat (g) per meal	**129.1**
Salt (g) per meal	**1.3**
Calories per meal	**2476**

chicken and chips

Fat (g) per meal	**95.7**
Salt (g) per meal	**1.9**
Calories per meal	**1903**

mushroom omelette and chips

Fat (g) per meal	**141.7**
Salt (g) per meal	**3.7**
Calories per meal	**2052**

salt
6g

fat
70g

vital statistics

These are the recommended daily amounts of calories, fat, saturates, salt and sugars that the diet of an adult man and woman should contain. They are for everyone and vital to you and your health – stay within them and you're on your way to leading a healthier life. Go above them and your weight will increase and place strain across your body.

calories
Men 2500
Women 2000
Children 1800

sugars
90g

fat
70g

saturates
20g

salt
6g

other cultures

A question: If every country around the world exists on basically the same diet – vegetables, meats, fruit, dairy products, grains etc – and they are prepared in much the same way, how is it that in comparison to say a Mediterranean or Asian diet, we as a nation seem to be that much more unhealthy?

The answer's quite straightforward and has a lot to do with how we treat the event of eating our food and how that food is prepared.

In Mediterranean countries food is an event to be enjoyed by family and friends, eaten at regular times and can often take up to two hours each evening to complete. It means that food is eaten over a longer period, the body has time to digest what is eaten and less food is consumed. Also, because the meal times are looked forward to, less snacking between meals takes place and if Mediterraneans feel the urge to grab a bite of something, it's more likely to be a piece of fruit or a packet of nuts.

How people shop is also different to how we now choose to do it here in the UK. Shopping abroad often includes visiting several places to buy each food, including local butchers and greengrocers, avoiding the pitfalls of buying processed food.

In Asia, most dishes are loaded with vegetables, with meat added to accompany them. In comparison, we often do things in reverse, with meat being the mainstay around which the rest of our dish is made. In parts of Japan – known to be amongst the healthiest nations in the world – they stop eating when they are almost full, instead of pushing on until everything is eaten.

The story is the same across the world. If food is freshly prepared and rich in vegetables, and if you give yourself time to eat it slowly and therefore eat less, the benefits to you and your health become more pronounced.

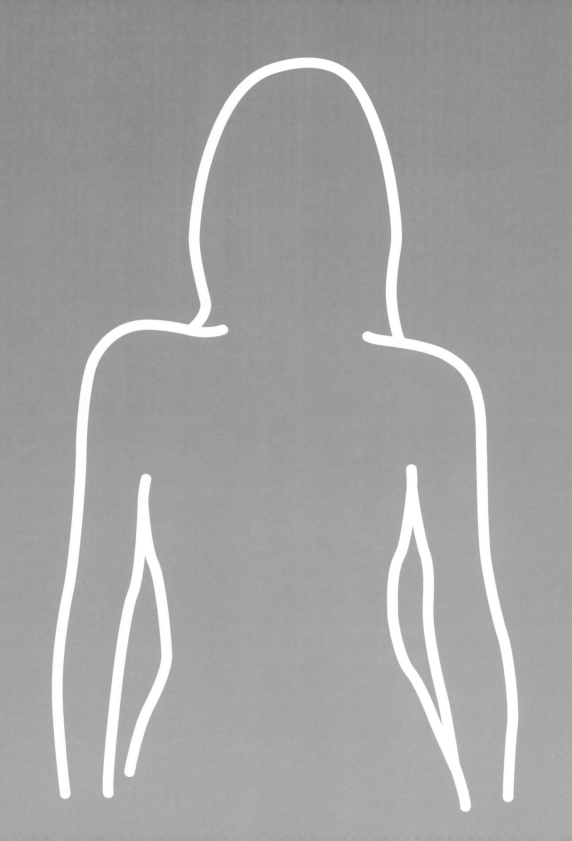

chapter 2

nutrition

Good nutrition is of vital importance to our health. Nutrition is a system of healing that uses fluids, diet, therapeutic techniques and vitamin supplements to treat you as an individual. So, if a client has thyroid problems, exercise may be prescribed as it helps tissues use the thyroid hormones. It treats the cause, not the symptoms and recognises that both the mental, emotional and physical states must all be treated for lasting health and happiness.

By applying the principles and methods of natural nutrition, not only do our ailments clear up and our bodies start working better, but we feel better. We become more confident; our self esteem improves; our thoughts have more clarity and we can become more creative. Our lives work better. Ultimately, it helps us become more dynamic, feel vital and – most importantly – happier.

One of the fundamental principles of nutritional therapy is that the body never ever works against us. It's always trying to do the best it can, with the conditions and materials it's given. So it follows that if you change the conditions and materials, the body will change.

a few words about cells

The human body is composed of approximately 70 trillion cells. These cells make the tissues that make the organs that make us. So, whatever is going on at body level is also going on at a cellular level. If you've got low energy, your cells have low energy. Depressed? That cell is depressed too. It's important then to recognise that fundamentally, your cells are you.

The cell goes through a day / night cleanse ritual, and if you look at the diagram you'll see the cleansing pattern of a healthy cell.

Healthy body cells are made up of about 70% water, and brain cells 80%. They're surrounded by a semi-permeable membrane, made primarily of Essential Fatty Acids (50% in the body and 60% in the brain). This cell membrane is very important in letting nutrients in and toxins out.

During the day, sodium (Na) – whose natural place is outside the cell – moves into the cell, bringing hydrogen with it. This changes the pH balance (power of hydrogen) of the cell, making it more acidic. To counteract the acidity, calcium enters the cell and makes it contract. These two minerals are called electrolytes, and push the potassium and magnesium out of the cell.

At night, when we're resting, the magnesium and potassium push back into the cell, making the cell relax. The magnesium in particular gives the cell energy and is a vital part of the cleansing pattern.

Simplified cleansing pattern of a healthy cell

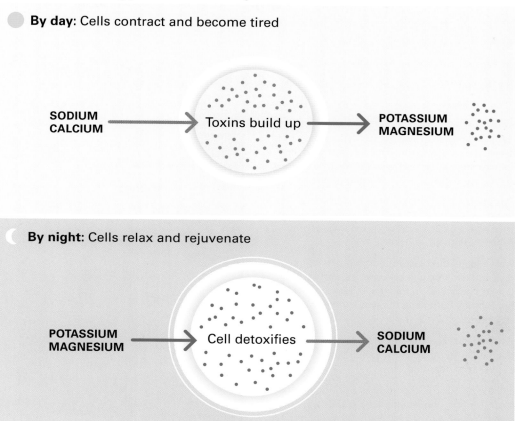

By day: Cells contract and become tired

SODIUM
CALCIUM → Toxins build up → POTASSIUM
MAGNESIUM

By night: Cells relax and rejuvenate

POTASSIUM
MAGNESIUM → Cell detoxifies → SODIUM
CALCIUM

Typically by day, our cells can toxify as they change their chemical make up. By night, the process is reversed and if you stay hydrated, the cells repair themselves ready for another day's work. In order to reduce toxicity and maintain hydration you need to drink plenty of water during the day.

One of the easiest ways to tell if your cells aren't completing the cleansing ritual is how you feel when you wake up in the morning. Do you wake up in the morning feeling sluggish and groggy? If it takes you a bit of time to come round, and you wake feeling tired, then that's a sure indicator of an incomplete cleanse. If you're waking up full of beans, happy and ready to go, then your cells are doing nicely.

A toxic cell is dehydrated, has an impaired membrane, and is unable to hold the electrolytes in the correct place. In short, it's unable to work to its potential. Does that sound like you?

Cells are amazing things and deserve to be looked after and treated as well as you do. They are committed to doing the best they can, so imagine their potential if they were given the right materials to do their job. The possibilities are endless.

On the following pages we make a few suggestions for small changes you can make – centring on water, linseeds and flaxseeds – to encourage your cells to throw off their toxicity and work more effectively.

water
the drink of choice

Nutrition and health are vast fields and with so much new and contradictory information from so many sources they can be a bit overwhelming. So, where do you start? Water is our starting point.

Our bodies are made up of approximately 70% water – pure, clean still water. So it's crazy that so many of us don't drink enough water and overdo it with other drinks.

Water keeps our bodies hydrated and feeling well and can't be gained from tea, coffee, fizzy drinks, cordial, flavoured water, juices or alcohol. Remember, it must be the best quality water we can afford.

We tend to take water for granted, yet water is the means through which nearly every function of our body operates.

It is the primary component of all bodily fluids; blood, lymph, digestive juices, urine, tears and sweat. Water is involved in almost every bodily function, from circulation and digestion to the absorption and elimination of wastes. Without clean water, we struggle to create a healthier balance in our lives.

Water is relaxing, soothing, moistening and cooling.

Dehydration is not just caused by not drinking enough water, but by emotional stress, poor diet, environmental factors like air travel, mobile phones, radar, everyday household chemicals, smoking, licit and illicit drugs and inherited toxicity. In fact, anything that causes you stress is dehydrating. So you can see how important it is to consume plenty of water.

Dehydration
Dehydration is implicated in scores of health problems, from diabetes and angina to colitis, hiatus hernia, high blood pressure, headaches, high cholesterol, migraines, asthma, allergies, depression, low mood, stress, arthritis, weight problems, eczema, low energy and Irritable Bowel Syndrome (IBS) (Bathmanghelidj).

The water challenge:

Most of us know we should drink more water. But there are all sorts of reasons why we're not, including some of these thoughts:

- water's boring
- I'll be in the toilet all the time
- it's a fallacy; plenty of people are 'well' and don't drink water
- there's no way I could drink that much water
- I can't function without tea / coffee / alcohol

But once you start drinking water it becomes harder not to drink, as the benefits are so great.

Why not challenge yourself to drink four pints/ two litres every day for two weeks? Halve your other fluid intake and see how you feel. By that time you'll be feeling better, and can start to reduce your other fluid intake even more. And if you're not thirsty all the time, you won't want so much tea / beer / fizzy pop anyway.

The reason that we recommend four pints a day is that our body uses four pints every day in its metabolic processes. We need at least those four pints, just to stop dehydration increasing.

There's been lots of discussion lately about the four pint rule and whether it's true or not. See for yourself – try drinking more water for a few weeks, and decide whether it's true for you. You're the only one who can know how you're feeling.

The lives we lead and the environment that most of us live in are stressful, so it's vital that we're consuming enough water to help our bodies function to their full potential.

The type of water we choose is very important – unfortunately, the water coming out of our taps is not in the greatest condition, but there's also controversy over bottled water and the amount of empty bottles it leaves behind. Just do the best you can – a pint of any sort of water is still better than coffee, tea, booze or fizzy pop.

Water filters are a good way of avoiding buying lots of bottled water, and all of the extra packaging it creates. They filter out impurities like heavy metals and chlorine, and are a handy way of storing water, either chilled in the fridge or at room temperature.

Water drinking tips

- Start your day with a pint of water first thing in the morning. This is when you're at your most dehydrated, as your body has been working overnight to complete its day / night cleanse.

- Water is best drunk warm; the body holds it in the stomach until it reaches body temperature, before distributing it. The closer it is to body temperature, the faster you become rehydrated.

- Try and replace your morning cup of coffee or tea with a cup of hot water. If you're really struggling you can put a slice of lemon in your hot water, but drinking hot water on its own is a good habit to get into. It's not a question of how the water tastes, it's what it does for you.

- Don't drink with meals – or up to 45 minutes after a meal – as fluids dilute your stomach acid and stop you digesting food thoroughly, which is key to our health and well being.

The change will be easier than you think and you'll get to the point where you'll wonder how you ever managed without water.

flaxseeds/linseeds

Let's get one thing straight. Flaxseeds and linseeds are the same thing; people call them by either name for different reasons, and suppliers may package them differently. But it's the same seed, so don't spend hours searching for them both in your local supermarket. For the purpose of clarity, we'll call them linseeds here.

Linseeds have abundant levels of Omega 3 and Omega 6 Essential Fatty Acids, in a perfect balance, which are readily assimilated by the body. EFAs are vital, as they can't be manufactured by the body and so must be obtained by our diet.

Linseeds are nature's richest source of Omega 3, which is needed to make prostaglandins, the precursors to our feel good hormones. We tend to get enough Omega 6 in our diets, but our Omega 3 is woefully lacking.

Linseed tea is also rich in lignans, which contain anti-cancer properties and are great for balancing our hormones. Soaked linseeds and linseed tea are the best ways to start bringing Omega 3 into your body.

Linseeds are nature's laxatives; they lubricate the bowels, nourish the spleen, pancreas and immune system. They also:

- Help to regulate weight and bowel function
- Are successful in lowering cholesterol
- Improve immunity and reproduction
- Useful in degenerative disorders

A small warning; linseeds may not be appropriate for everyone, particularly those with chronic bowel problems such as colitis, diarrhoea, diverticulits, IBS (particularly if there is a lot of diarrhoea), so think about supplementing with psyllium husk. Your colon is responsible for dumping faecal matter, reabsorbing water and the electrolytes sodium, potassium, calcium and magnesium. It's crucial to the healthy function of our bodies: it's as long as we are tall, the diameter is equal to our wrist.

Your colon will like linseed tea (which is basically thickened water, and the next step up from soaked linseeds in terms of the EFA content) because flax is a natural laxative. It also lowers cholesterol, regulates weight and improves immunity, amongst other things.

You can get flaxseeds / linseeds from some supermarkets, health food shops and online.

Preparing and taking linseeds

Soak two tablespoons of linseeds overnight in half a pint of water. Take one tablespoon first thing in morning with your first pint of water of the day. Take the other tablespoon last thing at night with just enough water to swallow the linseeds. Repeat it every day.

Soaking linseeds is important as it brings the oil out of them and helps the body to absorb the oil. The texture of the soaked linseeds can be a little unusual – it might feel a little strange when you first swallow soaked linseeds, but it soon gets easier. Just drink them down – it tastes unusual at first, but you'll get used to it.

Linseed Tea

This might sound quite longwinded to start off with, but the benefits are worth it we promise.

Place two tablespoons of linseeds in a pan with a litre of boiling water.

Bring to the boil.

Turn off, cover and leave for 8–12 hours.

Put them back on the heat on the smallest ring with the lowest heat and let them cook through for one hour. Strain the seeds out while the water's still hot, and drink as soon as possible. This can be made and consumed every day.

food and mood

Diet is obviously the next step and is very important in helping you feel healthier and happier. This book is dedicated to taking you in the right direction. In purely nutritional terms, some foods stand out – we talk more about them and give you some recipes to try out from page 39 onwards.

Food not only affects our body and how it works, but has a massive effect on our mental wellbeing. Blood sugar is crucial for our mental state – even simple changes help. Low blood sugar, or hypoglycaemia, can be caused by exercise, not eating regularly and even using our brain too hard. If our blood sugar drops too low, we feel as if we've got no energy, or can't think properly.

The body and brain need a certain amount of sugar to function normally – when we eat, our blood sugar level increases and the body produces insulin to make cells take in sugar. If you're healthy and eat sensibly, your blood sugar stays fairly constant throughout the day. But if you have a meal that stimulates the body to produce too much insulin too quickly, your blood sugar level may decrease rapidly and lead to feelings of low energy, tension and, in extreme cases, aggression. The effect is magnified when you drink alcohol with your meal – alcohol stimulates insulin release and can exacerbate the sudden drop in blood sugar.

But the brain is a complex machine and it's rarely one single factor that links food and mood. As well as the type of food we eat, low serotonin levels can lead to increased insulin production and associated low blood sugar.

Serotonin is a chemical released in the brain, which allows nerves to fire and transmit messages through the body. Serotonin makes you feel happy and helps us sleep, stay calm and relieves depression. It helps the body regulate many functions, including mood, aggression, appetite and sexual desire. Low serotonin levels are believed to be linked to mild depression and many anti-depressants work by increasing the amount of serotonin available to the brain.

So, although the science behind food and mood is complicated, there's plenty of evidence to show that eating a healthy balanced diet is important for our mental well-being. Sugary snacks and drinks may be marketed as giving the body a psychological and physical boost, but it's not actually the case. Walking for ten minutes can make you feel more energetic than eating a high-energy bar – the psychological boost from a sugary snack usually only lasts for 10 – 20 minutes. So if you want to feel better for longer, ditch the snack and hit the track.

10 instant mood boosts

1. Stretch
Reach up as high as you can. Breathe deeply, stand on your tiptoes and stretch out your fingers. It feels great.

2. Stroke a dog / cuddle your cat
Experts reckon having a pet can add years to your life through the calming, therapeutic effect of curling up with them. Not to mention all the dog walking.

3. Listen to your favourite song
On the bus, in the privacy of your house or driving to work – sing along at the top of your voice and you'll smile instantly.

4. Laugh
Whether it's talking to someone you know makes you laugh or watching a funny film, laughter not only relieves physical tension, but releases feel-good chemicals in your brain.

5. Wear bright colours
No wonder we all feel less cheery in winter, with dark mornings and long nights. Pick a piece of clothing in a colour that makes you smile.

6. Get out more
Whether you're at home or at work, if you're feeling down – or are about to explode – step outside for a break. Just a walk around the block'll make you feel better. Stand up straight, look up, breathe deeply. Maybe even fly a kite.

7. Have a bath
Not only is it warm and relaxing, having a bath is serious 'me time'. Light some candles, fill up on foam bath, and soothe your stresses away.

8. Dance around the house
Sashay from room to room or wiggle while you're washing up. Just getting moving's not only good exercise, but will soon put a smile on your face.

9. Plan something exciting
From your next holiday or an adventure day to a night in or out with your nearest and dearest, having something to look forward to is a massive mood boost.

10. Breathe
That's it. Just breathe. Shut the door, then sit with your back straight, close your eyes, and breathe deeply. Just concentrating on your breathing will banish everything else from your mind.

skin brushing

These few changes are starting to make a difference to your body now, as you're giving it the tools it needs to cleanse itself. The body cleanses, detoxes and nurtures itself every second; you're just helping it along now, instead of impeding its natural rhythms.

Once the cells, tissues and organs start throwing out all of these toxins, they need somewhere to go. They come out through the bowel, skin, kidneys and the lungs, but if you've been dehydrating your body for years, these routes will be a bit stagnant and need a helping hand. That's where the therapeutic techniques come in.

The first technique to mention is skin brushing.

Skin brushing is the act of brushing dry skin with a natural bristle brush and is usually done prior to a shower or a bath.

Why skin brushing?
The skin is the body's largest organ of elimination. 10% of all body waste should come through the skin, and skin brushing aids this process.

In a toxic body there's a lot of congestion, and the routes to elimination will be blocked or sluggish, so it's imperative that we help the toxins leave our bodies in as painless a manner as possible.

Not only does skin brushing help the physical removal of toxins, but it has a great effect on our mental and emotional states too, because it feels so good.

Skin brushing removes the stale acid mantle – a combination of sweat and sebum – from the skin, unblocking the pores and allowing the body to dump toxins through the skin. It also encourages the renewal of skin cells and aids the circulatory system.

How to skin brush
On a dry body, start underneath your feet and work up the feet, legs and abdomen with firm strokes. Brush as vigorously as is comfortable. Brush up the arms, bottom and back; brush across the shoulders and down the neck. Brush down towards breast level.

The whole process should take four or five minutes. It's best to follow with a bath or shower, and preferable in the morning. You'll really notice that your skin feels alive.

But we know that changing your habits can be a big ask. If you can't do it every day, do it whenever you can – have a nice five minutes to yourself, and you'll still feel better for it.

summary

If it sounds like there's a lot to take in, then there are a few things to remember to help you along. Start with small steps – if you're struggling to drink four pints of water a day, then start with two, and build up slowly. And, as with everything we suggest in the book, it's a gradual process of change. If you don't get to your target one day, pick it up again the next.

Use your friends and family to support your changes – rely on your friends, partner or a work colleague, or – if possible – get professional nutritional advice. You could also try keeping a diary of what you eat and drink, so you can relate changes in your body and emotions back to it. Listen to your body – it knows what it needs.

It's quite usual to feel a change in your emotions too; you're changing your life, but this is the beginning of a great adventure. Enjoy it.

ten
fantastic foods

1 Linseeds
Linseeds are the richest plant source of Omega 3 fats, which are essential for a healthy brain, heart, joints and immune system.

2 Sea vegetables
Sea vegetables like wakame, dulse, hijiki, nori, kelp and arame have up to 20 times the mineral and vitamin content of land vegetables and are a good alternative to salt for seasoning. Some also encourage the removal of heavy metals from the body.

3 Leafy greens
Kale, cabbage, chard, collards, spinach, watercress and other members of the leafy greens family are loaded with magnesium, the 'relaxing' mineral. They're also great sources of calcium, iron, potassium, vitamin C and vitamin A.

4 Sprouts
And we're not talking brussels here... sprouts (alfalfa, mung, sunflower, aduki, buckwheat, lentils etc) are young green plants germinated from seeds of any living vegetation. They're full of antioxidants, which protect our bodies from degeneration, and are a fabulous source of protein. Vitamins increase by 500% overall when seeds are sprouted. B vitamins increase by as much as 2000%.

5 Nettles
They're free, and they clean up your blood! Try making nettle tea or putting some in a soup.

6 Quinoa
Quinoa (pronounced Keen wah), is a seed that can be used as a grain. It's a complete protein, so has all of the essential amino acids within it. It's a great alternative to meat, as animal produce is usually cited as the only source of complete protein.

7 Almonds
The best of the nuts, almonds contain good quality fats in the form of Omega 6 and have a high protein content. Soak them before eating and they become crunchier and more digestible.

8 Beetroot
Great in soups, salads or juiced, beetroot cleans our blood and is high in antioxidants. The leaves of the beets can also be eaten... a two-in-one veg.

9 Short grain brown rice
The Chinese call it the 'food of the colon'. The name might not be snappy, but it aids elimination, mops up acidity and is rich in B vitamins, which are good for lowering stress and giving you energy.

10 Lentils and Pulses
A cheap and cheerful source of protein, and infinitely kinder to our bodies than meat.

chapter 3

<u>food</u>

We won't even start on all the technical terms like saturated fats, trans fats or polyunsaturated fats because to most of us they're just words without an awful lot of meaning. So, to move away from all of that, our guide to eating more healthily is quite straightforward. It's about avoiding processed, additive-dominated foods and understanding that the more you're tempted to eat fast foods as opposed to foods you've prepared yourself, the more your health is likely to be adversely affected.

How you shop is important. Farm shops, local fruit and veg stores and butchers play a big part, as their food is more likely to have been sourced locally and you'll be able to ask questions about its freshness and origin, plus advice on preparation and cooking.

Then there are the supermarkets. Of course, nearly everyone shops at a supermarket and they too provide healthy foods, but again it's about buying the freshest produce and avoiding processed and frozen foods where you can.

local and seasonal

Buying locally from local suppliers – who can demonstrate their knowledge of food and the produce they sell – fits with being and staying healthier. There's a great deal to be said for knowing where your food's come from before you buy it.

We advocate finding local farm shops that are steeped in the expertise of producing and selling fresh meat and vegetables. Through their enterprising know-how they're often much more like a delicatessen, selling the condiments you'll need to create all sorts of meals and foods you may never have tried before.

The Yew Tree Farm Shop is local to us; they're a great example of a farm turning their premises into a food experience. They produce their own meats and as much as possible they source all of their produce locally, often from other farms and suppliers they know personally.

Graham, Ann and their staff have worked hard since 1981 to turn their family owned former traditional farm into a destination of choice for thousands of food lovers each year. Full of domestic and farm animals, the grounds of the shop make it an ideal place to spend time with friends and family, chatting to the staff, enjoying the country atmosphere, and getting to know more about the food you buy.

We want you to shop locally, buy local produce and enjoy doing so – farm shops are often a bit of an adventure and as their foods change seasonally (as they should), each visit can offer you something new to try.

Ann has provided us with her grandmother's recipe for you to try – we have and it makes an amazing Sunday lunch. You'll find the recipe on page 98.

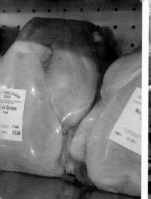

GOOSE EGGS 75p each

YEW TREE FARM SHOP

the countryside on your doorstep

eating out

Eating out can sometimes be every bit as unhealthy as eating the takeaways we introduced earlier. The food is usually prepared in the back somewhere and we've got no idea what goes into some of the meals we pay for.

Eating out is a vital ingredient of a balanced healthier life – giving you great food, atmosphere, laughter and enjoyment – with friends or family, or both.

Everyone has a favourite place to eat, a place you trust and want to go back to time and time again. Ours is the Everyman Bistro, the oldest and most popular in Liverpool – so they've got something right.

The owner and inspiration, Paddy Byrne, will tell you he 'got into food by accident', but his mantra is 'good food is a right for everyone' – so he built a bistro of iconic proportions.

With Tom, his head chef, the Everyman's starting point is good quality food, locally sourced and served fresh everyday. Not for them the 'you eat what we serve' ethos; it's more a case of 'you eat what you see'. The menu is presented before you at the counter, so you can see the quality of the ingredients before you buy your meal – it's the type of food you can trust almost as if you've put it together yourself.

They have great staff, who know their food and are open for you to test them on their knowledge. As Tom puts it, 'at the Everyman, it's not about "cheffing", it's all about cooking' – and you can taste that he means it.

Our point is that there are places like the Everyman throughout the country – restaurants, cafés and bars which care about the food they're selling, and go that little bit further to bring you the best meal they possibly can. So when you find one, support it, and visit it as much as you can.

Next time you're out try our Eating Out test. Wherever you are – ask the questions, watch the staff and enjoy the food. And if it doesn't measure up, move on.

Healthier Eating Out test

- Is the food prepared fresh everyday?
- Are most of the ingredients sourced locally?
- Are the staff friendly, knowledgeable and passionate about what they do?
- Is the owner always looking to improve?
- Is the chef accessible and ready to chat?
- Is the food the same great standard all the time?
- Does the atmosphere feel like it's all about you and your enjoyment?

kitchen cupboards

There are several ingredients that crop up time and again in the recipes we've chosen for this book. We don't want you to have to run out and buy scores of new ingredients each time you want to try a new dish, so here are a few pointers for stocking your cupboards.

Herbs

Herbs will keep fresh for about three days in your fridge; some harder herbs, like thyme and rosemary, will last a bit longer – your best bet's to freeze any herbs left over. Our chef Tony suggests putting any unused herbs in the freezer and pulling them out when you need them. His advice is not to use them in salads though, but to save frozen herbs for hot dishes like curries.

Olive oil

Some of our recipes specify extra virgin olive oil, while others don't. Use extra virgin for dressings or food that you're only lightly warming, otherwise it can lose its taste. Good extra virgin olive oil has a really peppery flavour, although if you're heating it up too much, you might lose the delicate taste.

Salt and pepper

We tend to talk about salt and black pepper: sea salt is easier for our bodies to digest, and tastes better, but you will find that it's more expensive than your normal kitchen salt. We recommend Malden sea salt, but if you can't afford it or choose not to buy it, normal salt's fine.

We do tend to insist on ground black pepper though. If you use your own ground black pepper you can taste the freshness, and it's got a more potent taste; there's also not much difference price-wise.

Butter

If you buy salted butter then there's no need to buy anything different for these recipes. From a chef's point of view, they often use unsalted butter as it means they can control the salt going into the dish, but you won't really notice any other difference.

Mustard

We use Dijon, English and wholegrain mustards in our recipes, as each has a different taste and texture. It's worth keeping a couple of different types in stock – they do last, keeping for about a year in the fridge.

Nuts and seeds

Nuts and seeds will also last a long time if you make sure they're stored in a sealed container once you've opened the packet. You can put them in a glass jar; we use the sealed containers you get from the takeaway for ours.

Kitchen kit

The equipment used in the preparation of these recipes is pretty simple – the one thing that we have used time and time again is a griddle, but if you haven't got one, you can simply grill your food instead. Griddles are good because they reach such a high temperature that you can dry cook your food on it; just rub a little bit of oil onto the meat, and the fat will run down in the grooves of the pan, so your food's not cooked in lots of fat.

The only other thing that you need is a decent knife; we recommend that you have two – a large one for chopping, and a smaller one for your veg.

summary

We've said it several times already, and we'll say it again – if you can, try and eat local seasonal food. Not only will it be in a great fresh condition when you buy it, but you'll get great variety in your diet from eating seasonal foods.

In putting this book together we've met stacks of people who're passionate about food; growing it, preparing it, and cooking it. Why don't you find someone who is too who'll inspire you to try different foods and recipes. They might be your greengrocer or the person on the fish counter in your local supermarket. Don't shop on autopilot – try and taste different things, and enjoy your food.

top ten food tips

1 The whole point of cooking for yourself is that you know exactly what's going into your dinner.

2 Write a shopping list before you go, so you know what you're looking for and don't forget key ingredients.

3 Shopping at your local butcher or fishmonger will allow them to advise you on the best cuts of meat or fish for the dish you're preparing, and they'll prepare your food for you if you're not confident about skinning, pinning or boning it.

4 Food may traditionally have been stored in a larder, but we heat our homes more now... Keep perishables like your veg in the fridge.

5 We throw out a crazy amount of food; once you get into the habit of preparing your own food, you'll soon be in the habit of using all sorts of leftovers in your fridge to create new recipes.

6 Try and buy seasonal food; it'll be ripe and ready to eat when you buy it, and fits in with the seasons you're preparing your food for. You'll also find a much wider range of food than you're used to finding in the supermarket.

7 Buying local food cuts down on the number of planes and trucks crossing the globe to deliver your food, and it's less likely to have been frozen and suffocated in layers of packaging to make it last until it reaches the supermarket shelves.

8 Build up a good stock of herbs, spices and condiments in your cupboard, so you don't have buy stacks of ingredients each time you want to try a new dish. Store them properly and they'll last for ages...

9 Shop with a bottle of water and some sugar-free gum; if you shop while you're hungry, you'll buy all sorts of convenience foods for instant gratification.

10 Be adventurous: each time you go shopping, try and buy something that's not on your usual list of 'staples'. Then think of a different and interesting way to use it...

chapter 4

recipes

One of the best things about cooking at home is that you get to see all of the ingredients that are going into your dish before they become a meal – it's your dish and it's up to you how much or how little of something you want to put in. We have prepared these recipes which are healthier and taste great, it's up to you to tweak them and make them even healthier – if you want to.

① mushroom and poached egg on griddled toast

Serves 1 or 2

You'll need two pieces of toast per person. Multiply the ingredients accordingly if you're cooking for more.

Ingredients

2 thick slices of good rustic bread
1 large field mushroom
2 free range eggs (must be very fresh or they'll fall apart when you poach them)
2 tsp fresh thyme leaves, finely chopped
2 tbls extra virgin olive oil
1 small handful watercress
1 tsp vinegar
Salt and freshly ground black pepper

Method

Firstly mix the olive oil and thyme together and brush the oil over the mushroom and the two slices of bread.

Preheat the grill and cook the mushroom until it's nearly done (2–4 minutes), then turn off the grill and leave the mushroom under it to keep warm.

Bring a pan of water to the boil, add the vinegar, then heat a griddle pan until it's smoking hot and griddle the bread on both sides until cooked; keep it warm under the grill with the mushroom.

Turn the heat down slightly on your pan of water and crack an egg into a cup; gently tip it into the water and repeat with the second egg. Simmer the eggs for 2–3 minutes then remove them with a slotted spoon.

Put your bread onto a plate, slice the mushroom in two and put half on each slice, along with an egg on each and the watercress to garnish.

② chilled spring porridge

Serves 1

Ingredients

75g rolled oats
200ml water
150g low fat yoghurt
1 tbls plump sultanas
1 tbls runny honey
1 banana, sliced
1 apple, cored
4 strawberries, quartered

Method

Place the rolled oats in a large bowl and stir in the water. Leave to soak for 30 minutes, and then drain off any excess liquid. Now add the yoghurt, honey and sultanas, and grate the apple into the bowl and mix well. Add the sliced banana and strawberries, then mix and serve.

③ grilled bacon and avocado bagel

Serves 1
**You'll need 1 bagel per person.
Multiply the quantities accordingly if
you're cooking for more.**

Ingredients
**4 rashers streaky bacon
8 good slices avocado
1 malted seed bagel, sliced in half
3 tsp crème fraiche
1 tsp fresh dill, chopped
Salt and freshly ground black pepper**

Method
Place the bacon and bagel on a grill pan and cook under a hot grill until the bacon is crisp and the bagel is golden.

Meanwhile, mix the crème fraiche and dill together and season.

Spread the crème fraiche over the cooked bagel, then place the bacon on one side of the bagel, with the avocado on top.

Repeat with the other side and serve open.

④ fresh pancakes with raspberries and passion fruit

Serves 2

Ingredients
**130ml semi skimmed milk
1 egg
Zest from 2 limes
30g melted butter
2 drops vanilla extract
1/2 tsp baking powder
1/2 tbls caster sugar
125g plain flour
10 raspberries
1 passion fruit
2 tbls low fat Greek yoghurt**

Method
Mix together the milk, egg, lime zest, butter and vanilla in a bowl, then whisk in the sugar, baking powder and flour until the batter is smooth.

Using kitchen paper, wipe a non-stick frying pan with a little oil, and on a medium heat drop one large tablespoon of the batter into the pan and cook for just under a minute on each side until golden brown. Do as many as you can fit into the pan without them touching each other, then remove.

Divide the pancakes between two plates and serve each with five raspberries and one spoon of yoghurt, then cut the passion fruit in half and scoop out the flesh over the top.

5 scrambled eggs and grilled tomato on muffins

Serves 1
Multiply the ingredients accordingly if you're cooking for more.

Ingredients
1 large tomato
2 free range eggs
1 tsp crème fraiche
1 wholemeal muffin, sliced in half
1 tbls fresh chives, chopped
1 tsp unsalted butter
Salt and freshly ground black pepper

Method
Slice the tomato in half and season with salt and pepper, then cook under a hot grill for about 5 minutes until soft.

Crack the eggs into a bowl and whisk in the crème fraiche and season with salt and pepper.

Put a pan on the heat and add the butter, then add the eggs and stir over a medium heat until they're starting to stiffen, but still look creamy.

Remove from the heat and stir in the chives. Toast the muffin and serve on a plate with the eggs on top and half a tomato on each.

6 spinach frittata (flat omelette)

Serves 4

Ingredients
100g spinach, shredded
3 tbls olive oil
8 eggs
6 spring onions, finely sliced
120g low fat cottage cheese
2 tbls fresh parsley, chopped
Salt and freshly ground black pepper

Method
Heat one tablespoon of olive oil in a large frying pan and add the spinach; cook gently for 2–3 minutes until soft, then set aside.

Crack the eggs in a bowl and mix well, then add the spinach, spring onions, cottage cheese and parsley and season to taste with a little salt and pepper.

Heat the remaining olive oil in a large frying pan and pour the egg mixture into it. Cook the omelette by pulling the edges gently in with a spoon over a medium heat for 3–4 minutes. Finish by carefully placing the pan under a hot grill for 30 seconds; serve with warm bread, or on its own.

7   avocado salad

Serves 2

Ingredients

2 large ripe avocado pears
Squeeze of lemon
100g cottage cheese
1 tbls fresh dill, chopped
5 tbls Greek yoghurt
1 clove garlic, crushed
1 green chilli finely chopped
Handful mixed lettuce leaves
Salt and freshly ground black pepper
Smoked paprika to garnish

Method

Cut the avocado in half lengthways around the stone and twist apart. Remove the stone and scoop out the flesh keeping the shells intact, then rub the inside of the shells with the lemon juice and set to one side.

Chop the avocado flesh up roughly and put in a bowl along with the cheese, chopped dill, yoghurt, garlic and green chilli. Season and mix well.

Place some of the salad leaves in each of the avocado shells and spoon the cheese mixture into each. Finish with a pinch of smoked paprika and serve.

8   green leaf salad

Serves 4

Ingredients

2 handfuls mixed green leaves
2 handfuls mixed coloured leaves
1 handful alfalfa sprouts (if you can get them)
3 tbls olive oil
1 tbls lemon juice
1 tsp Dijon mustard
Salt and freshly ground black pepper

Method

Mix together the olive oil, lemon juice and Dijon mustard in a bowl; season with salt and pepper, then put the salad leaves in a large bowl and drizzle over the dressing.

Mix carefully and serve in a large bowl or individually, and sprinkle over the alfalfa sprouts.

9   tomato and mooli salad

Serves 2

Ingredients

1/2 mooli, peeled and thinly sliced
3 tomatoes, sliced thinly
1 red chilli, deseeded and finely diced
2 tbls red wine vinegar
1 tbls olive oil
1 tsp honey
2 tsp soy sauce
2 spring onions, shredded
1 tbls fresh coriander, chopped
Salt and freshly ground black pepper

Method

Mix the vinegar, honey, olive oil and soy sauce in a bowl, then add the mooli and leave for 10 minutes.

Arrange the tomatoes on to a plate, and season with salt and pepper. Now pile the marinated mooli on top of the tomatoes and scatter the chilli, coriander and spring onions over the top.

10 asparagus and green bean salad with poached egg

Serves 4

Ingredients
100g green beans, trimmed
100g asparagus, trimmed
4 fresh free-range eggs
1 tbls white wine vinegar
3 tbls olive oil
1 tbls sherry vinegar
1 tsp Dijon mustard
1/2 red onion, peeled and finely diced
1 tbls fresh tarragon, chopped
Salt and freshly ground black pepper

Method
Bring a large pan of water to a rapid boil and add the green beans. After 2 minutes add the asparagus and cook for a further minute, then drain and put back in the empty pan with the lid on (off the heat) to keep warm.

Meanwhile, bring a pan of water to the boil and add the white wine vinegar. Cook one egg at a time by cracking into a cup, then swirl the water with a spoon and carefully lower the egg into the middle of the water. Poach for 3–4 minutes and remove and drain on a clean kitchen towel.

Mix together the olive oil, mustard, sherry vinegar, red onion and tarragon, and season. Divide the green beans and asparagus between four plates and place a poached egg on top, then drizzle over the dressing.

11 courgettes and egg on toast

Serves 2–4

Ingredients
4 good slices of French stick
6 tbls olive oil
1 large handful fresh basil, chopped
2 tbls grated Parmesan
1 clove garlic, crushed
1 tbls lemon juice
1 large or 2 small courgettes, grated
2 free range eggs

Method
Put the bread onto a baking sheet and drizzle with two tablespoons of olive oil, then bake in the oven gas at mark 5 / 190°C for about 5 minutes. Remove and keep warm.

Heat the remaining olive oil in a frying pan and add the courgettes; cook for about 3 minutes on a medium heat, then add the basil, parmesan, garlic and lemon juice and cook for a further 2 minutes. Season and set aside.

Meanwhile, bring a pan of water to simmering point and place the eggs in the water. Bring the pan back to a simmer and cook for 3–4 minutes, then remove the eggs from the pan. Peel them and slice in half.

To serve, divide the courgette mixture between the slices of French stick and place half an egg on top.

(12) houmous and watercress

Serves 2–4

Ingredients

400g can chickpeas, rinsed and drained
2 tbls olive oil
2 cloves garlic, crushed
2 tbls tahini (sesame seed paste)
Juice from 1 lemon
Salt and freshly ground black pepper
Water
$1/2$ tsp smoked paprika
1 bag watercress

Method

Place the chickpeas, olive oil, garlic, tahini and lemon juice in a food processor and blend until nearly smooth (you want a little texture). Add water little by little, until you get the consistency you want.

Season with salt and pepper and put in a bowl, then sprinkle over the smoked paprika and serve.

To eat, scrunch up watercress into a ball and dip in the houmous – it's a bit messy but lovely all the same.

(13) babaganoush with crispy pittas

Serves 4–6

Ingredients

2 aubergines
Juice from 1 lemon
1 clove garlic, crushed
3 tbls olive oil
2 tsp ground cumin
2 tbls Greek yoghurt
Salt and freshly ground black pepper

Method

Prick the aubergines with a fork and put them on a baking tray. Rub one tablespoon of the olive oil into them and bake in a pre-heated oven at gas mark 5 / 190°C for 30–35 minutes until soft. Remove and allow to cool.

When cool, slice in half and scoop out the flesh. Put the flesh in a food processor along with all of the other ingredients and blend until smooth. Season to taste and serve with grilled crispy pitta breads.

(14) spicy tomato salsa with celery sticks

Serves 4–6

Ingredients

400g tin good quality chopped tomatoes
10 cherry tomatoes, quartered
1 red onion, peeled and finely chopped
1 clove garlic, crushed
1 tbls fresh parsley, chopped
1 tbls fresh dill, chopped
1 tbls tomato purée
1–2 small green chillies, finely chopped with seeds
Salt and freshly ground black pepper
6 sticks celery, cut into batons

Method

Place all of the ingredients minus the cherry tomatoes and celery sticks in a bowl. Mix and slightly mash with a fork. Stir in the cherry tomatoes, season to taste and serve.

(15) guacamole with carrot sticks

Serves 4–6

Ingredients

3 ripe avocados, peeled and stone removed
4 mild chillies, deseeded and finely diced
2 tomatoes, deseeded and finely chopped
1 small white onion, peeled and finely grated
Juice from 1 lime
2 tbls fresh coriander, chopped
4 carrots, cut into batons
Salt and freshly ground black pepper

Method

Place all of the ingredients except one avocado in a bowl and mash them together. Slice, then cube the last avocado and fold into the mixture; season to taste and serve with chopped carrots.

16 chilled gazpacho

Serves 6–8

Ingredients
800g ripe tomatoes, peeled and chopped
1 cucumber, peeled and chopped
3 red peppers, deseeded and chopped
1 red chilli, deseeded and chopped
2 cloves of garlic, crushed
2 medium red onions, peeled and chopped
2 tbls red wine vinegar
100ml extra virgin olive oil
250g fresh white bread crumbs
250ml cold water
Salt and freshly ground black pepper

Method
Place the tomatoes, cucumber, peppers, garlic, chilli, breadcrumbs and onions in a food processor and puree until almost smooth, leaving some texture. Stir in the olive oil and vinegar, mixing well, and put in the fridge for 2 hours.

Once the soup has been in the fridge for 2 hours and has chilled, stir in the chopped parsley and season with salt and freshly ground black pepper and serve.

17 pea, roasted garlic and mint soup

Serves 4–6

Ingredients
1 whole head garlic
1 tsp olive oil
1 litre vegetable stock
10 spring onions
900g frozen peas
20 leaves fresh mint
Salt and freshly ground black pepper

Method
Slice the garlic in half and place the two halves in some kitchen foil, then drizzle with olive oil and cover with the foil. Bake the garlic in the oven for about 45 minutes on gas mark 4 / 180°C until soft and sweet, then remove the flesh and set aside.

Heat the stock in a large pan; add the peas and mint and bring to the boil, then cook for about 5 minutes. Remove the pan from the heat and add the spring onions and garlic, then drain the peas, reserving the stock.

Put the peas in a food processor and puree, adding enough of the stock to get a smooth consistency. Season with salt and black pepper and serve.

18   spinach soup

Serves 4–6

Ingredients

1 large onion, peeled and chopped
1 tbls olive oil
2 cloves garlic, crushed
200g floury potatoes, peeled and diced
600ml vegetable stock
450ml coconut milk
2 tsp ground cumin
1 green chilli, deseeded and chopped
500g spinach leaves, chopped
Zest and juice of 2 limes
Salt and freshly ground black pepper

Method

Heat the olive oil in a pan and cook the onions gently for about 5 minutes until soft, then add the garlic, potatoes, stock, ground cumin and chilli and simmer for about 10 minutes.

Add half the spinach, coconut milk and lime zest and juice and cook for a further 10 minutes until the potatoes are soft, then put in a food processor. Add the remaining spinach and purée until smooth – you may have to do this in batches if the food processor is not big enough.

When the soup is done, season to taste and serve. The reason we add half the spinach raw at the end is because it helps to give a rich green colour and earthy taste to the soup.

19   chilled beetroot and orange soup

Serves 4–6

Ingredients

400g cooked but not pickled beetroot, chopped
300ml fresh orange juice
300ml cold water
500ml Greek yoghurt
4 drops tabasco sauce
2 tsp caster sugar
Salt and freshly ground black pepper

Method

Place the beetroot, orange juice, 3/4 of the water, yoghurt, tabasco sauce and sugar in a food processor and puree until smooth. Transfer to a bowl and put it in the fridge for at least 2 hours until chilled.

When ready to serve, add the remaining water if needed and season with salt and pepper. Serve in bowls with a couple of ice cubes.

20 salmon, pak choi and noodle soup

Serves 4

Ingredients

1.5 litres vegetable stock
2 tsp chopped fresh ginger
2 cloves garlic, crushed
2 lemon grass stalks, chopped
6 spring onions, finely sliced
3 tbls soy sauce
2 tsp sesame oil
400g salmon fillet, sliced into 8 pieces
A little olive oil
300g cooked egg noodles
4 small pak choi, leaves separated
1 small red chilli, deseeded and finely diced
80g bean sprouts
Salt and freshly ground black pepper

Method

Put the stock in a large pan and add the ginger, garlic, lemon grass, half the spring onions, soy sauce and sesame oil. Bring to the boil and simmer for 45 minutes. Strain the liquid into a clean pan, season to taste and keep on a low heat.

Heat a griddle pan until very hot; brush the salmon with the olive oil and cook on the griddle for 1–2 minutes on each side, then remove and set aside.

Put the pak choi leaves in the hot stock for 3 minutes, then divide the pak choi, noodles, chilli, bean sprouts, remaining spring onions and salmon into four bowls. Pour over the hot stock and serve.

21 watercress soup

Serves 4

Ingredients

1 large white onion, peeled and chopped
1 tbls olive oil
200g floury potatoes, peeled and diced
(Maris Piper are good)
600ml vegetable stock
200g watercress, chopped
2 tbls Greek yoghurt
Salt and freshly ground black pepper

Method

Heat the olive oil in a large pan and cook the onions slowly until soft but not coloured. Add the potatoes and stock and bring to the boil, then reduce the heat to a simmer and cook for about 20 minutes until the potatoes are soft. Take the pan off the heat and stir in the watercress, then put the lid on the pan and leave for 5 minutes.

Place the soup in a food processor and purée until smooth, then stir in the Greek yoghurt and season to taste. If the soup is too thick you can add a little milk or water before serving.

22

tuna niçoise

Serves 2 as a starter

Ingredients

200g fresh tuna, cut into strips
100g new potatoes
8 pitted black olives
4 anchovy fillets
50g cooked fine beans
6 cherry tomatoes, halved
1 hard-boiled egg, quartered
1 tbls fresh dill, chopped
2 tbls lemon juice
5 tbls extra virgin olive oil
1 tsp Dijon mustard
2 handfuls of watercress
Salt and pepper

Method

Place the potatoes in a pan of cold water and bring to the boil; reduce the heat to a simmer, cover and cook for 20–25 minutes. Remove the pan from the heat and put it in the sink, run the cold tap into the pan until the potatoes have cooled; drain and slice them into quarters.

Place the potatoes, olives, anchovies, beans and tomatoes in a bowl together. Mix the dill, lemon juice, olive oil and mustard in a separate bowl, season with salt and pepper, mix it into the vegetables, and set to one side.

Season the tuna with salt and lots of freshly ground black pepper and place under a hot grill for about 2 minutes on each side.

Put the watercress on a plate with the vegetables on top. Scatter the egg around, place the tuna over the salad, and serve while the fish is still hot.

23

salmon, watercress and pine nut salad

Serves 2 as a starter

Ingredients

300g salmon fillet, cut into 1 inch slices
8 asparagus spears
2 spring onions, finely sliced
2 good handfuls of watercress
2 tbls pine nuts
3 tbls extra virgin olive oil
1 tbls lemon juice
1 tbls fresh dill, chopped
Parmesan shavings to finish
Salt and freshly ground black pepper

Method

Season the salmon, then cook under a hot grill for about 1 minute on each side; remove and allow to cool.

Bring a pan of water to a rapid boil and cook the asparagus for 1 minute, then cool it down in a bowl of iced water or under a running tap.

When the asparagus is cool, pat dry and slice into 4–6 pieces. Put it in a bowl along with the spring onions and watercress, add the olive oil, dill and lemon juice, season and mix.

Place the salad on a large plate and break up the salmon over it. Scatter the parmesan and pine nuts on top and serve.

(24) thai green chicken salad

Serves 8–10 as a starter

Ingredients

3 chicken breasts, cooked and cooled
1/4 large red cabbage, shredded
1 red onion, peeled and finely sliced
1 cucumber, cored and sliced
2 carrots, peeled and sliced into matchsticks
100g mangetout, finely sliced
200ml coconut milk
3 tbls olive oil
3 tbls Thai green curry paste
1 tbls lemon juice
10 fresh mint leaves, shredded
1 large handful fresh coriander leaves, roughly chopped
Salt and freshly ground black pepper

Method

Roughly pull apart the chicken breasts into bite-sized chunks and put them in a bowl along with the red cabbage, red onion, cucumber, carrots and mangetout. Set to one side.

In a separate bowl, whisk together the Thai green curry paste and coconut milk, then whisk in the olive oil and lemon juice.

Add the coconut dressing to the salad and using your hands, mix thoroughly, then stir in the fresh mint and coriander. Season to taste and serve in a large bowl.

(25) haloumi, rocket and puy lentil salad

Serves 4–6 as a starter

Ingredients

250g haloumi cheese
200g rocket leaves
6 spring onions, trimmed
200g cooked puy lentils
1 red chilli, deseeded and diced
1/2 clove garlic, crushed
6 tbls extra virgin olive oil
1 tsp ground cumin
2 tbls lemon juice
1 tbls fresh coriander, chopped
2 tsp sesame seeds
Salt and freshly ground black pepper

Cooking puy lentils:
Simmer gently for about 30 mins
(or according to the packet's instructions)

Note:
Puy lentils may also be packaged as continental green lentils or Mediterranean lentils, so if you can't find them at first keep an eye out for those.

Method

Slice the haloumi into 1cm strips, then slice in half lengthways. Heat a griddle pan until it's smoking hot and carefully wipe a little oil onto it with a paper towel.

Griddle the haloumi for 1 minute on each side, then set it aside and keep warm. Now griddle the spring onions in the same pan for about 2 minutes, turning now and again, and set them aside too.

In a bowl, mix the olive oil, lemon juice, garlic, chilli and ground cumin together, then add the cooked puy lentils and mix well. Add the haloumi, spring onions, rocket and coriander and toss together, season with a little salt (not too much – the haloumi is very salty) and freshly ground black pepper.

Serve on a large plate and scatter the sesame seeds over the top.

26 caesar salad

Serves 2

Ingredients

1/2 clove garlic, crushed
6 anchovy fillets
1 egg yolk
1/2 tsp Dijon mustard
1 tbls lemon juice
100ml olive oil
2 tbls grated Parmesan
1 large cos lettuce
150g ciabatta
1 tbls olive oil
4 slices streaky bacon
Parmesan shavings
Freshly ground black pepper

Method

Place the garlic, 2 anchovy fillets, egg yolk, mustard and lemon juice in a food processor and blitz into a smooth paste. While you're blitzing, drizzle 100ml of olive oil in, until smooth and creamy. Stir in the grated parmesan and season with black pepper.

Slice the ciabatta into 2cm cubes, drizzle with 1 tbls of olive oil and bake in a hot oven gas mark 8 / 220ºC until golden. Meanwhile, grill the bacon on both sides until crisp and set aside – if you haven't got a separate grill, cook your bacon first and leave it to one side.

Tear the cos lettuce into large pieces and place them in a bowl, along with the ciabatta croutons; drizzle most of the dressing over it, mix well and place into a large serving bowl.

Place the remaining anchovies and the crispy bacon on top, drizzle a little more dressing on, and scatter the parmesan shavings on top to finish.

27 egg and watercress salad

Serves 2

Ingredients

8 free range eggs
6 spring onions, finely sliced
1/2 red chilli, deseeded and finely diced
2 good handfuls watercress
3 tbls olive oil
1 tbls lemon juice
1 tsp Dijon mustard
2 tbls fresh dill, chopped
Salt and freshly ground black pepper

Method

Place the eggs in a saucepan and fill with cold water, then bring to the boil, cover and remove from the heat. Let the eggs stand in the water for 10–12 minutes.

Peel and quarter the eggs and set aside; put the watercress on a large plate, then scatter over the eggs, chilli and spring onions.

Mix together the olive oil, lemon juice and Dijon mustard in a small bowl; season with salt and pepper, then drizzle over the salad. Finally, sprinkle the dill over it and serve.

28 mozzarella, parma ham and nectarine salad

Serves 4–6

Ingredients

2 large balls mozzarella
6 slices Parma ham
2 nectarines quartered and stoned
300g bag mixed lettuce leaves
10 black olives
10 sun blushed tomatoes
4 spring onions, trimmed and sliced
1 handful fresh basil leaves
Juice from 1 lemon
4 tbls extra virgin olive oil
Salt and freshly ground black pepper

Method

Heat a griddle pan (or a frying pan if you don't have one) and using a paper towel, lightly oil it. When the pan is hot, griddle the nectarines for about 1 minute on each side, then remove them from the heat and allow them to cool.

Arrange the lettuce leaves and basil on a large plate and then scatter over the black olives, sun blushed tomatoes and spring onions. Place the slices of Parma ham in and around the salad. Drain the mozzarella and tear each ball into four pieces, and add them to the salad.

Scatter the cooled nectarines over the top and season the salad with salt and black pepper; drizzle the lemon juice and olive oil over everything and serve.

29 poached salmon with fennel salad

Serves 2

Ingredients

2 salmon fillets (approx 200g each)
1 lemon, sliced
1 bay leaf
1 small bunch tarragon
2 cloves garlic, sliced in half
1 litre water
1 fennel bulb, thinly sliced
1 red onion, peeled and thinly sliced
1/2 tbls fresh tarragon, chopped
Juice from 1/2 lemon
2 tbls olive oil
1 tbls balsamic vinegar
Handful watercress
Salt and freshly ground black pepper

Method

Put the water in a pan, along with the sliced lemon, bay leaf, small bunch of tarragon and garlic. Bring to the boil, and then reduce to a simmer.

Season the salmon with salt and pepper, then place into the pan and cover; cook the salmon gently for 5 minutes, then remove from the heat and leave in the pan with the lid on for a further 3 minutes.

While the salmon is cooking, put the fennel and red onion in a bowl and add the fresh tarragon, lemon juice, olive oil and balsamic vinegar. Season to taste and serve on a plate with the salmon and watercress.

30 japanese chicken and cucumber salad

Serves 2

Ingredients

2 cooked chicken breasts, sliced
2 cucumbers, cored and very finely sliced
4 tbls rice vinegar
1 tsp caster sugar
2 tsp sesame oil
1 tbls sesame seeds
1 tbls fresh coriander, chopped
Pinch of salt

Method

Lay the cucumber on kitchen paper and gently squeeze out some of the moisture.

In a bowl, mix together the vinegar, sugar, salt and sesame oil, and stir in the cucumber, chicken and coriander. Serve on a large plate and sprinkle over with sesame seeds.

31 pea, ham and mint salad

Serves 2 as a starter

Ingredients

1 smoked ham hock, weighing about 1 kilo, soaked overnight
2 handfuls pea shoots (if you can get them)
300g frozen garden peas
1 red onion, peeled and finely sliced
2 little gem lettuce, shredded
1 small handful fresh mint, shredded
2 tbls cider vinegar
2 tsp Dijon mustard
1 clove garlic, crushed
5 tbls extra virgin olive oil
Salt and freshly ground black pepper

Method

Wash the ham and place in a large pan; cover with water and bring to the boil and simmer with the lid on for 2–2 1/2 hours, until the meat is really tender. Remove from the pan and leave to cool.

Bring a large pan of water to a rapid boil and cook the peas for 2–3 minutes, then drain the peas and run the cold tap over them (this stops them from cooking further and helps to keep their colour).

Mix the vinegar, mustard, garlic and olive oil in a small bowl; season and set aside.

When the ham is cool enough to handle, shred all of the meat off and place in a large bowl, along with the peas, red onion, lettuce and fresh mint. Add the dressing, then mix well and adjust the seasoning if needed.

Serve on a large plate with the pea shoots sprinkled over the top.

satay noodle salad

Serves 8

Ingredients

100g mangetout
150g beansprouts
2 red peppers, deseeded and sliced into strips
2 spring onions, finely sliced
500g cooked egg noodles
1 tbls sesame oil
1 tbls olive oil
1 tbls soy sauce
1 red chilli, finely chopped with seeds
50g smooth peanut butter
100ml coconut milk
2 tbsp lime juice
1 handful fresh coriander, roughly chopped
1 tbls sesame seeds
Salt and freshly ground black pepper

Cooking egg noodles:
Cook in boiling water for 3–5 minutes
(or according to the packet's instructions)

Method

Slice the mangetout in half lengthways and place in a large bowl, along with the beansprouts, sliced red peppers, spring onions and cooked egg noodles.

In a separate bowl, mix together the sesame oil, olive oil, soy sauce, chilli, peanut butter, coconut milk and lime juice. Add to the vegetables and mix well, season with salt and pepper, then stir through the coriander.

Serve in a large bowl with sesame seeds sprinkled over the top.

 ## beetroot and feta salad

Serves 6

Ingredients

6 large cooked beetroot
4 spring onions, sliced
100g rocket leaves
50g walnuts
125g feta cheese
2 tbls extra virgin olive oil
1 tbls red wine vinegar
1 tsp wholegrain mustard
1 tbls fresh dill, chopped
Freshly ground black pepper

Method

Slice the beetroot into French fry sized pieces and mix in a bowl with the spring onions, walnuts and rocket.

Put your salad on a large serving plate. In a bowl, mix together the olive oil, red wine vinegar, mustard and dill and season with black pepper. Crumble the feta over the salad and drizzle the dressing all over the salad.

34 spring lamb, broccoli and pasta salad

Serves 6–8

Ingredients

400g lamb leg steaks
300g dried orichette (or any pasta you like)
5 tbls extra virgin olive oil
2 tsp ground cumin
1 tsp smoked paprika
1/2 tsp ground turmeric
1 green chilli, deseeded and diced
1 clove garlic, crushed
3 tbls lemon juice
1 red onion, peeled and sliced
300g tender stem or purple sprouting broccoli
3 tbls fresh coriander, chopped
3 tbls fresh mint, chopped
Salt and freshly ground black pepper

Method

Firstly bring a large pan of water to a rapid boil and cook the pasta according to the instructions on the packet. When cooked, cool under cold running water and drain.

Brush the lamb with a little oil and cook under a hot grill to your liking; when it's cooked shred the meat and allow it to cool.

To cook the broccoli, bring a pan of water to the boil and cook for 2–3 minutes until tender; remove it from the heat and cool under running water, then slice each into three pieces.

Mix together the olive oil, cumin, paprika, turmeric, chilli, garlic and lemon juice, then add to a large bowl with all of the remaining ingredients and mix well.

Season with salt and freshly ground black pepper and serve on a large plate.

35 panzanella salad

Serves 2

Ingredients

150g ciabatta
5 tbls extra virgin olive oil
250g tomatoes
1/2 small red chilli, deseeded and diced
1/2 small red onion, peeled and thinly sliced
4 anchovy fillets, chopped
1 tbls capers, rinsed
1 small handful fresh basil, sliced
1/2 clove garlic, crushed
2 tbls red wine vinegar
Salt and freshly ground black pepper

Method

Tear the ciabatta into one inch pieces and put them on a baking tray. Drizzle over a tablespoon of the olive oil and season, and grill until part of the bread is golden brown. Remove and set aside.

Roughly chop the tomatoes and put them in a bowl – along with any of the juices – then add the onion, chilli, anchovies, capers and bread, and mix.

In a separate bowl, mix the remaining oil, vinegar and garlic; add this to the salad, along with the basil. Mix well and season to taste.

moroccan spiced couscous

Serves 8 as a side dish

Ingredients
400ml vegetable stock
230ml orange juice
140g dried apricots, chopped
1 yellow pepper, cored and cubed
1 red pepper, cored and cubed
1 green pepper, cored and cubed
1 red onion, peeled and finely diced
460g dry couscous
1 tbls ground cumin
2 tsp ground cinnamon
100g chopped almonds
50g chopped hazelnuts
1 handful chopped parsley
Salt and freshly ground black pepper

Method
Bring the stock and orange juice to the boil in a large pan; add the dried apricots and peppers and cook for 2–3 minutes. Remove from the heat and stir in the onion, couscous, cumin and cinnamon. Put a lid on the pan and leave for 10 minutes, off the heat.

After 10 minutes, fork through the couscous and stir in the almonds, hazelnuts and parsley. Season with salt and pepper and serve In a large bowl.

 mackerel and little gem salad

Serves 2–4

Ingredients
3 peppered smoked mackerel fillets, flaked
2 spring onions, finely sliced
1 tbls capers, rinsed and chopped
3 cornichons (small gherkins), chopped
1 hard boiled egg, chopped
1 tbls fresh dill, chopped
1 tbls lemon juice
3 tbls mayonnaise
2 little gem lettuce, leaves torn
$^1/_2$ cucumber, sliced
Salt and freshly ground black pepper

Method
Mix together the mackerel, spring onions, capers, cornichons, egg, dill, lemon juice and mayonnaise in a bowl, and season to taste.

Lay the lettuce leaves and cucumber on a large plate and spoon over the mackerel mixture; serve with crusty bread.

38 nutty coleslaw

Serves 4–6 as a side dish

Ingredients

$1/2$ small white cabbage, shredded
3 carrots, peeled and grated
3 sticks celery, shredded
1 large white onion, peeled and finely sliced
30g cashew nuts, chopped
30g almonds, chopped
3 tbls Greek yoghurt
2 tbls mayonnaise
1 tbls whole grain mustard
Juice from $1/2$ lemon
2 tbls fresh parsley, chopped
Salt and freshly ground black pepper

Method

Mix together the cabbage, carrots, celery, onion, cashew nuts and almonds in a large bowl. In a separate bowl, mix the yoghurt, mayonnaise, mustard and lemon juice; add to the coleslaw and mix well – get stuck in with your hands.

Season with salt and freshly ground black pepper and serve on a large plate with chopped parsley sprinkled over the top.

39 avocado and prawn salad with sauce marie rose

Serves 2

Ingredients

2 ripe avocado pears, peeled and sliced
450g cooked and peeled prawns
$1/2$ cucumber, sliced
3 spring onions, sliced
1 handful frisse lettuce
350ml mayonnaise
100ml tomato ketchup
1 tsp Worcester sauce
Juice from 1 lemon
3 drops tabasco sauce
2 tbls fresh chives, chopped

Method

Put the prawns in a bowl along with the mayonnaise, ketchup, Worcester sauce, lemon juice, tabasco and chives; mix well and season to taste.

Place the frisse on a plate and arrange the cucumber and avocado over the lettuce. Place the prawns on top and scatter spring onions over the dish.

40 potato salad

Serves 8

Ingredients

1.2 kg new potatoes
6 spring onions, finely sliced
2 tbls fresh dill, chopped
4 tbls mayonnaise
4 tbls Greek yoghurt
1 tbls lemon juice
1 tbls creamed horseradish
Salt and freshly ground black pepper

Method

Place the potatoes in a pan of cold water, bring to the boil and simmer for about 20–25 minutes until cooked. Drain the potatoes, and put them to one side.

When the potatoes are cool enough to handle, slice them in half and put them in a bowl. Add the spring onions, dill, mayonnaise, yogurt, lemon juice and horseradish, season to taste and serve.

41 waldorf salad

Serves 8–10

Ingredients

4 Braeburn apples
4 Granny Smith apples
250g celery, sliced
120g walnuts, chopped
250ml soured cream
2 tsp lemon juice
Salt and pepper
2 good handfuls of rocket
1 tbls curry powder

Method

Wash the apples and cut into quarters, then take out the core and cut into half inch cubes – place into a bowl along with the celery and walnuts. Mix in the soured cream, curry powder and lemon juice, season to taste and serve on a plate on top of the rocket.

42 baked chicken with boulengere potatoes

Serves 4

Ingredients

4 x chicken breasts
Juice and zest from 1 lemon
1 tbls fresh thyme, finely chopped
2 tbls olive oil
800g Maris Piper potatoes, peeled and finely sliced
1 white onion, peeled and finely sliced
150ml vegetable stock
Salt and freshly ground black pepper

Method

Layer the potatoes and onion in a shallow baking dish, seasoning between each layer; pour over the stock and cover with foil. Bake in a preheated oven at gas mark 4 / 180°C for 45 minutes, then remove and keep warm.

Meanwhile, put the chicken breasts in a bowl, along with the lemon juice and zest, chopped thyme and olive oil. Mix well and place in an oven-proof dish; cover with foil and bake in a preheated oven at gas mark 6 / 200°C for 25–30 minutes. Remove and serve with the boulengere potatoes.

43 lamb steak with roasted vegetables

Serves 2

Ingredients

2 lamb steaks (approx 200g)
Juice from 1/2 lemon
1/2 aubergine, cubed
1 courgette, cubed
1 red onion, peeled and cubed
8 cherry tomatoes
4 tbls olive oil
2 sprigs thyme
1 clove garlic crushed
2 tsp ground cumin
Salt and freshly ground black pepper

Method

Put the aubergine, courgette, red onion, garlic, cumin, thyme and three tablespoons of olive oil in a roasting tin, and cook in a preheated oven at gas mark 7 / 220°C for 20–25 minutes. After 15 minutes, stir in the cherry tomatoes and season with salt and freshly ground black pepper.

Put the lamb steaks on a grill tray and brush with the remaining olive oil. Season and squeeze over the lemon juice, then place under a hot grill for 4–5 minutes on each side. Slice the lamb and serve with the roasted vegetables.

44 steak and tomato salad

Serves 2

Ingredients

2 rib-eye steaks (approx 200g)
3 tbls olive oil
$^1/_2$ red onion, peeled and finely sliced
100g cherry tomatoes, halved
3 tomatoes, quartered
100g rocket leaves
2 tbls fresh dill, chopped
1 tbls balsamic vinegar
Salt and freshly ground black pepper

Method

Heat a griddle pan until hot, then rub one tablespoon of olive oil into the steaks and season with salt and freshly ground black pepper. Put them in the hot pan and cook for 3 minutes on each side for rare, or 4 minutes for medium. Remove the steaks from the heat and rest on a plate for ten minutes, covering them.

Put the onion and all the tomatoes in a bowl and add the remaining olive oil, balsamic vinegar and dill, then mix well and season. Mix in the rocket and serve on a plate with the steak sliced over it.

45 honey chicken with dill potatoes and grilled radicchio

Serves 2

Ingredients

2 chicken breasts, cut into strips
2 tsp whole grain mustard
1 tsp honey
Juice from $^1/_2$ lemon
4 tbls olive oil
300g new potatoes
1 tbls fresh dill, chopped
1 radicchio, quartered
1 tbls balsamic vinegar
Salt and freshly ground black pepper

Method

Put the chicken in a bowl along with the mustard, honey, lemon juice and one tablespoon of olive oil; mix well, season and set aside.

Put the potatoes in a pan and cover with cold water, then bring to the boil and simmer for 20–30 minutes depending on the size of the potatoes. Drain and slice in half, then add one tablespoon of olive oil and the dill and keep warm.

While the potatoes are cooking, put a griddle pan on the heat and turn the grill on to a medium heat. Put the chicken strips on a baking tray and place under the grill; cook for 4–5 minutes on each side or until cooked through – keep an eye on the chicken as the honey can burn easily. Brush the radicchio with the remaining olive oil and place on the griddle; cook for 3–4 minutes on each side and when cooked drizzle with the olive oil.

Serve the chicken on a plate with the dill potatoes and the griddled radicchio.

(46) grilled chicken with new potatoes and broccoli

Serves 2

Ingredients

2 chicken breasts, sliced in half
to make 4 flat pieces
2 tsp smoked paprika
1 tsp ground cumin
2 tbls olive oil
Juice from 1 lime
300g new potatoes
1 head broccoli cut into spears
Salt and freshly ground black pepper

Method

Put the paprika, cumin, olive oil and lime juice into a bowl and add the chicken; mix well and leave to marinate for 30 minutes.

Meanwhile, place the potatoes in a large pan and cover with cold water; place the pan on a high heat and bring to the boil, then reduce the heat and simmer for 20–30 minutes depending on the size of the potatoes. Remove and drain off the water.

While the potatoes are cooking, bring a pan of water to the boil and put a griddle pan on a high heat. When the griddle pan is hot, carefully place the chicken in it; season with salt and pepper and cook for about 5 minutes on each side. While the chicken is cooking, put the broccoli in the other pan and cook for about 5 minutes, until tender.

Serve the chicken on a plate with the potatoes and broccoli.

(47) irish stew

Serves 4

Ingredients

12 mutton chops
2 onions, sliced
400g chanteray carrots
3 large potatoes, peeled and sliced thickly
650ml chicken stock
1 sprig fresh rosemary
2 sprigs fresh thyme
2 tbls fresh parsley, chopped
Salt and freshly ground black pepper

Method

Remove any excess fat from the chops and place in a large casserole dish along with the onions, potatoes, carrots, thyme and rosemary. Pour over the stock, season well and mix.

Put the stew – with the lid on – in a pre-heated oven, gas mark 4/160 °C for 2–2 1/2 hours, then take out and remove any fat that has risen to the top with a spoon.

Stir in the chopped parsley and check the seasoning, then serve.

48 grilled sardines with chickpea, tomato and beetroot salad

Serves 2

Ingredients

4–6 sardines, gutted and cleaned
1 tbls fresh rosemary, finely chopped
1¹/₂ lemons
3 tbls olive oil
1 can of chickpeas, rinsed and drained
100g cherry tomatoes, halved
200g cooked beetroot, cubed (not pickled)
¹/₂ red onion, peeled and finely sliced
1 tsp ground cumin
1 tsp ground coriander
¹/₂ tsp ground cinnamon
¹/₂ clove garlic, crushed
1 tbls fresh coriander, roughly chopped
1 tbls fresh dill, roughly chopped
Salt and freshly ground black pepper

Method

Preheat the grill to its highest setting; place the sardines on a grill tray and brush with one tablespoon of the olive oil, then season and sprinkle over the rosemary and set aside.

Put the chickpeas, cherry tomatoes, beetroot and onion in a bowl, then mix in the ground cumin, ground coriander, ground cinnamon and crushed garlic. Now stir in the remaining olive oil, juice from one lemon, chopped dill and coriander. Season with salt and freshly ground black pepper and set aside.

Put the sardines under the hot grill and cook for 4–5 minutes on each side. Squeeze over the remaining lemon juice halfway through grilling and serve on a plate with the salad.

49 coconut and coriander crusted salmon with basmati rice

Serves 2

Ingredients

2 salmon fillets (approx 200g)
20g hazelnuts, crushed
30g desiccated coconut
1 tbls fresh breadcrumbs
1 tbls fresh coriander, chopped
2 tbls olive oil
Salt and freshly ground black pepper
150g basmati rice

Method

Mix the hazelnuts, coconut, breadcrumbs and coriander in a bowl, then season with salt and black pepper and stir in the olive oil.

Put the rice in a pan and cover with boiling water, then simmer with a lid on for 10–12 minutes, or until rice is tender. Drain and keep warm. While the rice is cooking, spoon the coconut mixture on top of the salmon fillets and place them on a baking tray.

Cook under a medium grill for about 8 minutes, until the crust is golden and the fish is flaky. Serve on a plate with the rice.

50 steamed salmon with fennel and peppers

Serves 2

Ingredients

2 salmon fillets (approx 200g)
1/2 red chilli, deseeded and finely diced
1 tsp finely grated ginger
1 fennel bulb, quartered
1 red pepper, deseeded and quartered
1 red onion, peeled and quartered
2 tsp ground cumin
3 tbls olive oil
2 tbls lemon juice
Salt and freshly ground black pepper

Method

Bring a pan of water to boil, and cook the fennel and onions for about 3 minutes, then drain. Put them in a bowl with the peppers, then add the cumin and one tablespoon of olive oil. Mix well.

Heat a griddle pan until extremely hot, then place the vegetables in it and cook until the peppers are tender and everything has good bar marks. Put the peppers in a bowl and season with salt and black pepper, and stir through the remaining olive oil and lemon juice. Set aside and keep warm.

While the vegetables are cooking, put some water in a steamer; bring to the boil, then turn down to a medium heat. Put the salmon fillets on a small piece of kitchen foil and season with salt and pepper, then spread the ginger and chilli on top.

Put the fish in the steamer with the lid on for 8–10 minutes, and serve on a plate with the vegetables.

51 marinated salmon with corn and pepper salsa

Serves 2

Ingredients

2 salmon fillets (approx 200g)
1 red chilli, deseeded and finely diced
Juice and zest of 1 lime
1/2 tsp runny honey
300g drained sweetcorn
1 red pepper, deseeded and diced
1 green pepper, deseeded and diced
1/2 red onion, peeled and finely diced
6 cherry tomatoes, quartered
3 tbls olive oil
Juice from 1 lemon
2 tbls fresh coriander, chopped
Salt and freshly ground black pepper

Method

Mix together the chilli, lime juice and zest, honey and some black pepper in a bowl, then add the salmon fillets and leave to marinate for 10–15 minutes.

Heat the grill until hot, and place the salmon fillets on a tray and cook under the grill for 2–3 minutes on each side.

Meanwhile, mix together the sweetcorn, red and green peppers, red onion and tomatoes in a large bowl, then stir in the olive oil, lemon juice and coriander. Season to taste and serve on a plate with the salmon.

52 tandoori salmon with cucumber and mint salad

Serves 2

Ingredients

2 salmon fillets (approx 200g)
8 tbls plain yoghurt
1 tbls hot paprika
1 tsp chilli powder
1 tsp ground cumin
2 tbls lemon juice
1 tbls olive oil
$1/2$ tsp ground turmeric
$1/2$ tbls tomato purée
1 tsp grated ginger
1 cucumber, deseed and cubed
$1/2$ white onion, peeled and finely diced
2 tbls fresh mint, chopped
1 handful watercress
Salt and freshly ground black pepper

Method

Mix together four tablespoons of yoghurt, the paprika, chilli powder, cumin, one tablespoon of the lemon juice, olive oil, turmeric, tomato purée and grated ginger in a bowl, then spread it over the salmon fillets and leave to marinate in the fridge for 30 minutes.

When the fish has marinated, drain off any excess marinade and place on a grill tray, under a medium hot grill and cook for 6–8 minutes on each side.

To make the cucumber salad, place the cucumber in a bowl, along with the remaining yoghurt, onion, mint and the remaining lemon juice. Season and serve with the fish on a plate with the watercress.

53 steamed fishcakes with pak choi

Serves 2

Ingredients

450g salmon fillet
1 tbls fish sauce
2 tbls light soy sauce
1 tsp grated ginger
Juice from $1/2$ lemon
1 red chilli, deseeded and finely diced
2 tbls fresh coriander, chopped
1 egg yolk
2 large pak choi, quartered
1 tbls olive oil
1 tbls oyster sauce

Method

Finely chop the salmon and place in a bowl, along with all of the other ingredients except the pak choi. Mix well, then divide into four and shape into patties.

Heat one tablespoon of olive oil in a pan and fry the pak choi on a medium heat for about 6–7 minutes. Add the oyster sauce and cook for a further minute; remove from the heat and keep warm.

Put the fishcakes on some greased foil and place in a steam pan; cook for 4–5 minutes, then remove and serve with the pak choi.

54 seared tuna with puy lentil salsa

Serves 2

Ingredients
2 tuna steaks (approx 200g)
3 tbls olive oil
50g puy lentils
8 cherry tomatoes, quartered
1/4 red onion, peeled and finely diced
1 red pepper, deseeded and finely diced
1 red chilli, deseeded and finely diced
2 tbls fresh coriander, roughly chopped
Juice from 2 limes
Salt and freshly ground black pepper

Method
To make the salsa, put the lentils in a small pan and cover with cold water, then bring to a gentle simmer and cook for about 30 minutes. When the lentils are cooked, drain off any excess liquid and put them in a bowl; while they're still warm, add the lime juice, two tablespoons of the olive oil and mix well.

Now add the tomatoes, red onion, red pepper and chilli; mix well and set aside to cool. Heat the remaining olive oil in a non-stick frying pan until hot, then season the tuna and put in the pan. Cook for 1–2 minutes on each side (this will leave the tuna slightly pink inside, so if you prefer it well done cook for longer).

Remove the pan from the heat, then stir the coriander into the lentils and season to taste. Serve the lentils on a plate with the tuna on top.

55 moroccan spiced cod with tabouleh

Serves 2

Ingredients
2 cod fillets (approx 200g)
1/2 tsp ground cumin
1/4 tsp ground cinnamon
1/2 clove garlic, crushed
1 small red chilli, deseeded and finely diced
1 tbls olive oil
100g bulgur wheat
3 spring onions, sliced
2 large tomatoes, chopped
1 small bunch parsley, chopped
1 small bunch mint, chopped
Juice from 1 lemon
3 tbls olive oil
Salt and freshly ground black pepper

Method
Mix together the cumin, cinnamon, garlic, chilli and one tablespoon of olive oil in a small bowl, then spread the paste over the cod fillets and set aside.

Put the bulgur wheat in a large bowl and cover with boiling water; leave to soak for 30 minutes and then squeeze out any excess water. Add the spring onions, tomatoes, parsley, mint, lemon juice and olive oil to the bowl and mix well. Season to taste and set aside.

Heat the grill until hot, and place the cod fillets on a baking tray. Put them under the grill and cook for 3–4 minutes on each side until cooked through. Remove from the heat and serve on a plate with the tabouleh.

asparagus and herb risotto

Serves 2

Ingredients

150g asparagus, trimmed
2 tbls olive oil
1 small red onion, peeled and finely diced
1 clove garlic, crushed
Zest from 1 lemon
1 tbls fresh parsley, chopped
2 tbls fresh dill, chopped
175g Arborio rice
75ml white wine
500ml hot vegetable stock
Salt and freshly ground black pepper
Parmesan shavings to finish

Method

Bring a pan of water to a rapid boil and cook the asparagus for 2–3 minutes; remove from the heat and put the pan under cold running water to cool the asparagus. Drain and set aside.

Heat the oil in a large pan and add the onions; cook on a medium heat for 5 minutes and then add the garlic – continue to cook for a further minute.

Add the rice and stir until all the rice is coated in oil, then add the wine and stir until the wine has been absorbed. Add a ladle of the stock and stir until almost absorbed – continue doing this until all of the stock has been used and the rice is tender.

Add the asparagus, herbs and lemon zest; season to taste and serve in bowls with the parmesan shavings on top.

 ## stuffed aubergines

Serves 2

Ingredients

1 aubergine
3 tbls olive oil
1 red onion, peeled and cubed
1 tsp cumin seeds
2 cloves garlic, crushed
3 tomatoes, chopped
1/2 tbls tomato purée
2 tbls fresh coriander, chopped
Salt and freshly ground black pepper

Method

Slice the aubergine in half lengthways; score the flesh and scoop it out, leaving a 1.5cm thick edge. Heat the oil in a pan and fry the onions and aubergine flesh for 5 minutes, then add the cumin, garlic, tomatoes and tomato purée and simmer for 5 more minutes.

Add the chopped coriander and season with salt and pepper, then spoon into the aubergine skins and place into an ovenproof dish. Pour about 200ml of hot water around them and bake in a pre-heated oven gas mark 6 / 200°C for 30–35 minutes.

Serve with salad.

58 steamed vegetables, noodles and cashew nuts

Serves 2–4

Ingredients
2 tbls olive oil
1 red onion, finely sliced
1 clove garlic, crushed
2 tsp grated ginger
500g broccoli
200g baby corn
100g mangetout
300g dried egg noodles
200g cashew nuts
1 tbls soy sauce
1 tbls sesame oil

Method
Bring a large pan of water to a rapid boil and cook the noodles for 10 minutes, then drain.

Put some water into a steamer and bring to the boil, then turn down to a medium heat and steam the broccoli, baby corn and mangetout for about 10 minutes until just cooked. Add the cashew nuts to the pan for 1 minute to warm through; serve in a bowl with the noodles and the soy sauce and sesame oil drizzled over the top.

59 hot carrot and cabbage salad

Serves 4 as a starter

Ingredients
300g white cabbage, shredded
2 tbls olive oil
2 red chillies, deseeded and diced
200g carrots, cut into matchsticks
$1/2$ tsp salt
1 tbls honey
1 tbls soy sauce
2 tbls rice vinegar
1 tsp sesame oil
1 tbls fresh coriander, chopped

Method
Heat the oil in a large pan and fry the cabbage and carrot for 2 minutes; add the chilli, salt and honey and fry for another 2 minutes. Add the soy sauce, vinegar, sesame oil and coriander, mix well and serve.

60 lamb kebab

Serves 2

Ingredients

1 lamb fillet or leg steak (approx 200g) sliced into 1cm strips
1/4 white onion, grated
2 cloves garlic, crushed
1 tsp ground cumin
1/2 tsp smoked paprika
3 tbls olive oil
Salt and pepper
Juice from 1/2 lemon
2 tbls Greek yoghurt
Handful mixed salad
2 pitta breads

Method

In a bowl mix together the lamb strips, grated onion, garlic, cumin, paprika and olive oil, then season with salt and freshly ground black pepper. Lay the lamb on a grill pan and place under a hot grill for 2–3 minutes on each side, then remove, squeeze the lemon over it, and keep warm.

Meanwhile, warm the pitta breads and slice along the tops to open up a pocket. Fill the pittas with salad and the lamb and finish with a spoon of yoghurt on top.

61 healthier pizza margherita

Serves 2

Ingredients

175g plain flour
1 tsp salt
1 tsp fast action dried yeast
1 tbls olive oil
120ml tepid water
200g can chopped tomatoes
1 clove garlic, crushed
1 tbls tomato purée
1/2 tsp caster sugar
1 tsp dried mixed herbs
1 ball buffalo mozzarella, drained and torn into pieces
10 basil leaves
1 tbls polenta
Salt and freshly ground black pepper

Method

Put the flour in a mixing bowl and add the yeast and one teaspoon of salt, then add the olive oil and water and mix using a spoon first and then your hands, until it forms a ball. Tip the dough onto your worktop and knead for 4–5 minutes, adding a little flour if it's too sticky to handle. Put the dough back in the bowl and cover with cling film; leave in a warm place for an hour, until it's doubled in size.

While you're waiting for the dough, make the sauce by putting the tomatoes in a pan, along with the garlic, tomato purée, sugar and herbs. Stir and heat gently until it thickens slightly, then set aside.

When the dough is ready, heat your oven to gas mark 8 / 220°C and put a large baking tray in. Remove the dough from the bowl and place it on a lightly floured surface; bash the air back out of it, then knead again for 1–2 minutes and shape into a ball.

Flour a rolling pin and roll out the dough until it's about 28cm in diameter, then take the baking sheet out of the oven and slide the pizza base onto it. Spread the tomato sauce over the base and dot the mozzarella and basil leaves all over it; season with a little salt and lots of freshly ground black pepper.

Put the baking tray in the oven and bake for 12–15 until the cheese is bubbling and the dough is golden. Leave to stand for a couple of minutes before serving.

chicken tikka massalla

Serves 2

Ingredients
400g chicken breast, cubed
2 tbls olive oil
200ml plain yoghurt
3 cloves garlic, crushed
2 tsp grated ginger
1/2 tsp chilli powder
3 tsp paprika
1/4 tsp ground coriander
1/4 tsp ground cumin
1 tsp garam masala
Juice from 1/2 lime
350g tinned tomatoes
1/2 tsp ground fenugreek
20g chilled butter
1/2 tsp vinegar
20ml single cream
2 tbls fresh coriander, chopped

Method
Mix together the yoghurt, garlic, ginger, chilli powder, two teaspoons of paprika, the ground coriander, ground cumin, 1/2 tsp garam masala, lime juice and a pinch of salt in a bowl. Add the cubed chicken, mix well and leave to marinate for 2 hours in the fridge.

Heat the oil in a large pan and add the chicken and the marinade, then cook on a medium heat for about 20 minutes, stirring until the chicken is tender.

In another pan, add the tomatoes and ground fenugreek, then cook for 5 minutes until some of the liquid has evaporated. Add the chilled butter, one teaspoon of paprika, half a teaspoon of garam masala, the vinegar and single cream, and cook for an extra minute. Add the sauce to the chicken, stir in the fresh coriander and season to taste.

Serve with boiled rice.

 ## prawn chow mein

Serves 2

Ingredients
225g dried egg noodles
3 tbls olive oil
1 yellow pepper, deseeded and sliced
100g chestnut mushrooms, sliced
6 spring onions, shredded
100g beansprouts
100g water chestnuts, sliced
250g peeled raw tiger prawns
2 clove garlic, crushed
2 tsp grated root ginger
2 tbls soy sauce
1 tbls oyster sauce
1/2 tsp Chinese five spice powder
2tbls rice wine or sherry
2 tsp corn flour, mixed with 2 tbls water

Method
Bring a pan of water to the boil and cook the noodles for 4–5 minutes, then put the pan in the sink and run cold water over it to cool the noodles down. Drain and set aside.

Heat the oil in a large frying pan or wok, then stir fry the pepper, mushrooms, spring onions, beansprouts, ginger, garlic and water chestnuts for 3 minutes on a high heat. Now add the soy sauce, oyster sauce, five spice and noodles, cook for 1 minute, then add the prawns, rice wine or sherry and the corn flour mixture. Continue to cook for a further 1–2 minutes and serve.

ann's grandma's orange-baked gammon

Serves 6–8

Ingredients
1¹/₂ kg (approx) gammon ham
2 oranges
2 tsp English mustard
2 tsp soft brown sugar
Crusty white bread / French stick to serve

Thanks to Ann at Yew Tree Farm Shop for this recipe.

Method
Soak the gammon for 3 hours in fresh, cold water to help draw out excess salt – you'll see the water become cloudy. Pre-heat the oven to gas mark 7 / 225ºC, and mix together the juice and rind from the oranges, the mustard and sugar while it heats up.

Leave the fat on the gammon and spread half of the mixture over it. Wrap the gammon in tin foil and put in a roasting tin in the oven. Cook for roughly 30–35 mins for every half kilo of weight – a 1¹/₂ kg gammon will need about 90–105 minutes. Half an hour before the end, take the gammon out. Unwrap it, remove the crackling from the ham, and score the fat underneath using a sharp knife. Rub the rest of the orange mix over the entire gammon and leave it uncovered for the rest of the cooking time.

Once cooked, remove from the oven, cover with foil and put a tea towel on top. Leave to stand for 10–15 minutes to draw the juices back in and keep it tender. Serve in chunks on crusty bread or as a roast.

 pam's healthier atthol brose (without whiskey)

Serves 6–8 (depending on size of serving glass)

Ingredients
1 large pot of plain yoghurt
3 punnets of fresh raspberries (or frozen raspberries, if you prefer)
220g jumbo oats (toasted)
3 tbls clear, runny honey
1–2 tbls caster sugar (to taste)

Thanks to Pam at the Everyman Bistro for this recipe.

Method
Firstly, pre-heat your oven to gas mark 7 / 225ºC. Leave eight raspberries to one side for a garnish. Crush the remaining raspberries with a little caster sugar to sweeten them – if you're using frozen raspberries, it's easier to defrost them first. Sprinkle the oats evenly across the baking tray or foiled grill pan and toast until golden brown, and leave to one side to cool.

Put the yoghurt in a mixing bowl, and – keeping a few toasted oats to one side as a garnish – add the rest to the bowl and fold them into the yoghurt. Pour over half the runny honey and fold gently – just a couple of times, to leave a rippled effect.

Now layer your desserts. Place a few raspberries in the bottom of each dessert bowl or glass, followed by a layer of the yoghurt, honey and oats. Repeat these layers until your bowl or glass is full, and chill until you're ready to eat them. Sprinkle on the toasted oats, and top with a raspberry.

(66) tom's spinach, salmon and ricotta lasagne

Serves 6–8

Ingredients

500g spinach, washed
500g ricotta cheese
6 x 140g salmon fillets
50g Parmesan cheese, grated
1 large onion, finely chopped
4 cloves garlic, crushed
4 tins of chopped tomatoes
1/2 tube of tomato purée
1 bunch fresh basil, chopped
1 box wholemeal lasagne sheets
1 pinch sugar
1 pinch nutmeg
2 tbls olive oil
Salt and freshly ground black pepper
Crisp green salad leaves to serve

Thanks to Tom at the Everyman Bistro for this recipe.

Method

Pre-heat your oven to gas mark 6 / 200°C, then add a little olive oil to a frying pan and place on a medium heat. Add the onion and fry until the onion softens slightly. Add the tomatoes, tomato purée, and sugar; bring to the boil and simmer uncovered for 15 minutes. While you're waiting for the sauce, break up the ricotta into small blobs; sprinkle it with the nutmeg and a little salt and pepper.

When the tomato sauce is nice and thick, add the basil and season. Turn the heat off, and blend the sauce until it's smooth or squash the lumpier bits with a fork.

Put the salmon fillets on a lightly-oiled tray and season. Put the tray in the oven for 8 minutes, before taking it out and leaving on one side to cool. Leave the oven on, but turn it down to gas mark 4 / 180°C.

Put a cup of water into a saucepan and put it on a medium heat. Put the spinach into the pan, squashing it in if you have to. Leave over the heat until the leaves wilt; once it has wilted, remove the pan from the heat, drain and run under a cold tap to cool them down enough for you to squeeze out any excess water. Place into another mixing bowl.

Flake the cooled salmon fillets into the spinach bowl with a fork and mix it in gently – you don't want to break up the salmon too much more. Now layer your ingredients, starting with half of the salmon and spinach mix; cover them with lasagne sheets. Pour half of your tomato sauce on top and sprinkle over half of the Parmesan. Layer half of the ricotta and nutmeg on top and repeat the layers in the same order.

Bake in the oven for 25–30 minutes until golden brown on the top. Allow to stand for 5 minutes before serving with a fresh green, crispy salad.

summary

We're not going to ask you to give up your favourite food to start your healthier journey. We've included a broad range of different meats and fish, vegetarian options and old favourites, but you will have noticed that there's a lot of fish recipes. It's lean, can be steamed, poached or grilled – all healthier methods of cooking – it's good for you, and most of us don't eat enough of it.

Aside from that, we've tried to give you choices – an alternative way of cooking your favourite foods that might make them a bit healthier, and introduce you to something new. And then we threw in some gorgeous, mouthwatering photos. We hope they inspire you.

top ten foodie tips

1. Leave the salt until last. Taste your food and then season it, don't just add it automatically.

2. Whenever possible always use olive oil rather than vegetable oil or sunflower oil; olive oil is less refined.

3. Official advice suggests we should eat at least two portions of fish a week, including one portion of oily fish. The average Briton eats only a third of a portion per week.

4. Try and grill or griddle your food, so that the fat runs out of the food and away as you cook it.

5. Eating your Five a Day of fruit and veg is important but often a bit hard to achieve. Start with consistently eating three a day and get yourself into that routine and then add another portion as you feel you are ready.

6. If possible, steam your veg. Boiling veg sucks the nutrients out into the water, which we usually just pour away...

7. Eat slowly; chew your food properly and taste it more. You'll eat less, and enjoy what you do eat much more.

8. It takes your brain 20 minutes to understand that your stomach is full, but you can eat lots in a 20 minute sitting – slow down and eat slowly.

9. Make the preparation part of the cooking process. Don't see preparing your food as an inconvenience – invite friends round and enjoy the process.

10. Experiment. Use these recipes as a guide, but be brave; move ingredients around as you get to know what you like.

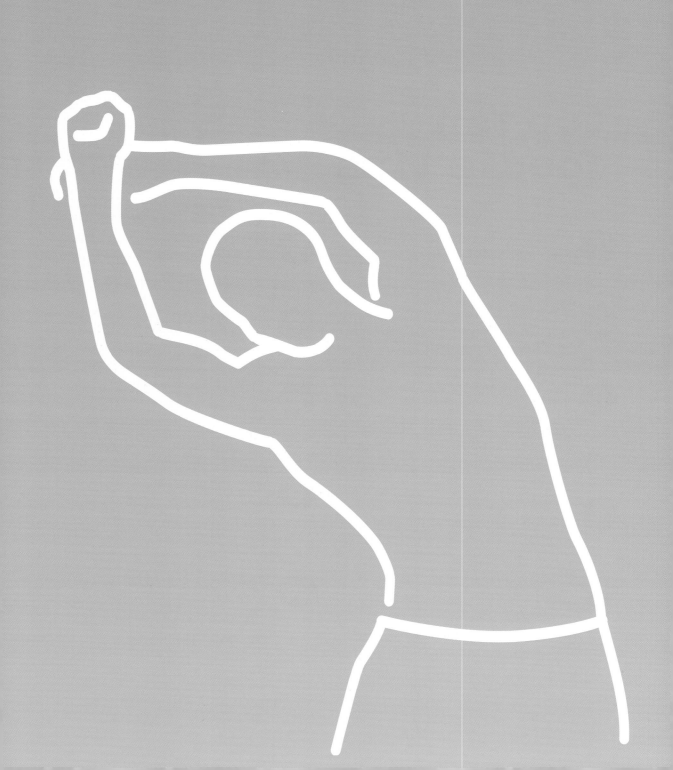

chapter 5

exercise

You wake up in the morning – you've got to get the kids to school and there's a full day ahead of you. You've got to pick the kids up again, find time for your partner and friends, feed your family, feed your friends, feed yourself; plan the following day, find time for a hobby. And then you have to think about exercise – something's got to give. Or has it?

Exercise plays a crucial role in your overall wellbeing. You can reduce all of those things that add on the pounds or give you a hangover, but without some form of exercise, we think you're missing out on something that can really improve your energy levels, your state of mind and generally how you feel about yourself. Our bodies weren't designed to sit around and be idle, so, while modern life has taken away many of the pressures that used to force us to be lean and fit, we need to make sure we're not seizing up through lack of use.

Like everything else in the book, this section is really just to get you to look through the exercise window. Use it to choose some small steps towards including more regular exercise in your everyday life. Again, we've set out to provide you with tips and advice to let you pick a route that suits – if you already exercise, then you'll know most of what we are suggesting. If you don't, some of what you're about to read will be new and a bit of a challenge. If you do stick with it, and find aspects of exercise you enjoy and that fit with your lifestyle, we promise it'll all be worth it.

motivation and routine are key

If you recognised yourself while you were reading the introduction to this chapter, you could say that you're already motivated, and used to completing lists of tasks in a busy life. And of course you are – but when it comes to adding something new and potentially difficult (at first) to that list, a different motivation is required – one that relies on planning and goal setting.

In most cases, motivation – or the lack of it – is the major blockage to starting a new or improved fitness routine. You've got to want to do it, otherwise there'll always be something to distract you. Like most things in life, motivation and routine are the keys to success when it comes to exercise.

Motivation is something that sparks inside us all and once triggered can help you achieve whatever goals you've set. It drives your ambition, increases your initiative and strengthens your desire to improve everything that matters to you. Sounds great, but what does it look like and how do you get there?

Much of what is written about the lack of motivation centres around your state of mind and how you behave – you may have lost faith in your own ability or how you look; you may not be that interested in much of anything anymore, and become a bit tetchy; you may feel that you never have the time to pursue an interest or potential hobby; or – let's face it – you may have just become a bit lazy all round. It's a place that most of us find ourselves in at some point in our lives – the trick is to acknowledge it and want to do something about it.

Becoming motivated and increasing your motivation is all down to you. We wish we could provide you with a quick fix answer, but getting there is all your doing. You'll need to give yourself time to sit down and set out some goals. You'll then need to break down those goals into tasks and concentrate on achieving them one at a time and then you'll need to practise and practise a bit more. Routine and small achievements will increase your motivation levels. It's not that difficult, but only you can do it.

And remember, training your body to start a new habit is always difficult, but it will soon become enjoyable. It's not as bad as you think.

endorphins

Endorphins are a family of chemicals produced in the brain by the pituitary gland and the hypothalmus; they're the brain's natural painkiller and three times more potent than morphine. The word itself is a combination of 'endogonous' and 'morphine', implying that endorphins are morphine-like substances originating from the body.

Endorphins are part of a chemical family known as 'neurotransmitters', which relay signals between the brain and the body. They signal the brain to start a variety of processes, from our perception of pain and psychological state to gastric and cardiovascular systems. How do we produce it, and why?

What happens when we exercise?

Endorphins are released when we undertake relatively long, continuous workouts of fairly high intensity where breathing is difficult, like running, swimming, cycling and football. The duration of the exercise is important, so short, strenuous exercise – like sprinting or tennis – is less likely to result in the brain releasing endorphins. Studies have shown that exercise is equally as effective at releasing endorphins in old and young people, and in those who have or haven't exercised regularly, so it's never too late to start.

Endorphins are our natural painkillers: long workouts can increase our pain threshold by about 30% because of the analgesic effect of the chemical. The pain-relieving effect lasts for about an hour after we stop exercising. Such is its potency that one study even demonstrated that moderate exercise mitigated the pain of women in labour. It's also been reported that increased endorphins can help relieve back pain.

Regular exercise can reduce psychological tension and even cause euphoria. In fact, some studies have shown that exercise is as effective at treating certain types of anxiety, depression and eating disorders as some medicines, because the chemicals released are so important to the brain.

Endorphins have also been linked to a decrease in blood pressure, and there's evidence to suggest that exercise and endorphins can boost our immune system too.

Food

Endorphins can also be released by eating certain types of food. The relationship between what we eat and how our brain responds is complex, but the food we eat triggers the production or release of certain chemicals in the brain.

Despite their reputation as 'bad foods', several studies show that eating carbohydrates makes us feel happier, and that diets low in carbohydrates are detrimental to mood.

Conditions like seasonal affective disorder (SAD) and PMS are associated with increased consumption of foods with a high fat or carbohydrate content. Food cravings are also common in times of stress, particularly for women, and people who constantly diet are more likely than people who don't to eat more when they're stressed.

Chocolate is the most commonly craved food when we feel stressed, and certain foods – often high in fat and carbohydrate, like chocolate, cheese and cream – can induce the release of endorphins, making us feel better. That's why we crave and eat the wrong type of food when we're feeling down.

Alcohol also affects endorphin release and therefore our mood. Moderate alcohol consumption increases the level of endorphins, which is why we often feel happier after a few drinks. But habitual alcohol use leads to a deficiency in endorphins and people susceptible to alcoholism may have naturally low endorphin levels.

energy boosts

Food plays a pivotal energy-boosting role in your exercise routine. To compliment the effort we hope you're going to put in, we've created a recipe that's easy to prepare, full of taste and will help you train. Try this super smoothie to start your day. Another great energy boosting recipe is steamed vegetables and noodles on page 93.

banana and mango smoothie

Ingredients
$1/2$ **mango**
$1/2$ **banana**
$1/2$ **small cup of apple juice**
(try not to use concentrate)
1 passion fruit
$1/3$ **small cup of orange juice**

Serves 1

Method
Peel the mango and chop it a bit before putting it into the blender. Peel and add the banana (eat the other half while you're making it). Strain the passion fruit into the blender (but don't add the seeds), then add the apple and orange juice. Whizz it all up and pour into a glass with a little ice – it's great.

setting goals – it takes time

Goal setting allows you to sit down and visualise what you'd like to achieve from your exercise. It's about deciding on your ultimate goal and then working back from the time you think it will take for you to achieve it. Then it's about splitting your goal up into do-able chunks, so that you can measure your progress.

The reasons for exercise, your goals, can take many forms and we've included a list of those that have driven us, or we know are regular incentives for people to exercise.

You can download it from our website at www.cancookwillcook.org.uk

Reasons to exercise

- I've had a big health scare, or someone very close to me has. It's now or never if I'm going to start making some changes to my life.

- I want to lose weight: I can feel the pounds gathering in all the wrong places. The challenge is to get back to the shape of a few years ago.

- I want more energy: to spend more time with the kids, get out for walks, ride a bike...

- I have a wedding / holiday coming up: I want to fit into that dress / suit / bikini and feel good with everyone watching.

- I want to run a 10k – it may take a few months but it can be done.

- I want to have a social life, but still become fit and healthier.

- I don't feel confident in my appearance and I know it's holding me back from doing things I enjoy.

- I used to take being fit and healthy for granted, but I was really shocked last week when I ran for the bus / ran up the stairs how hard I found it.

getting started:
exercise begins at home

Not everyone has a gym nearby. Even if you do, you might decide that a gym isn't for you, you can't afford it, or just want to use your money for other priorities. So, we've come up with some suggestions to help you fit exercise into your life more easily – either at home or in the park.

On the following pages, our personal trainer Clare demonstrates exercises she uses with her clients as she takes them through her starting off routine. They can be replicated at home or in the park.

We should say something here about seeking your doctor's advice before you embark on any new fitness routine, but we hope too that you'll be responsible enough to realise the importance of fitness on your long-term health, and take responsibility for yourself.

training zone –
the scale of 1 to 10

The programme we've put together is designed to increase your fitness and provide you with exercises that will result in general toning and increase your flexibility. But – as with everything in life – it requires a bit of effort.

Everyone's effort levels are different, depending on your ability and previous levels of training. The training zone we're suggesting can be used by everyone and is a tool to aid your progress. It's simple and can be used as part of your training sessions. Using it, the scale allows you to choose the right training zone for you.

The scale from one to ten relates solely to the effort you're expending during training.

If you're only on level one you're exerting no effort whatsoever – you simply haven't started.

If you're on your personal ten – your maximum effort – you're at your peak, training at a level you can't maintain for long. It's a period we suggest should be no longer than 10 seconds.

Your mid-point is five. Level five is your comfort zone, where you're exercising, but have yet to really exert yourself.

Above level five is about moving into your training zone. Ideally, you need to be between levels six and eight. Once you're here, your body temperature increase starts; you start to sweat, your heart rate increases and your breathing becomes deeper, but you should still be able to hold a conversation. This is where we suggest you maintain your training levels.

exercising at home

First you should consider what you will need.

A space
- Your lounge – in front of the TV
- On the landing with your favourite music turned right up
- Your bedroom – again with the TV or music as part of your motivation

Getting comfortable
- Exercise mats are perfect – easy to roll out and easy to store away again

Your equipment
- A set of dumb-bells: they're so flexible and are a must for all of the arm exercises. Dumb-bells weighing 1kg up to 5kg are perfect to start off with. Find your ideal weight before buying.
- An exercise ball: ideal for a multitude of exercises.

Exercises
Clare will demonstrate a number of exercise routines over the next couple of pages. You can also download exercises for your triceps and biceps from our website www.cancookwillcook.org.uk

training zone – at home

1+2. Single arm row (upper back)

Stand over your exercise ball with your chin in line with your chest. Keep your abdominals pulled in, and balance one knee on the ball, keeping your supporting leg soft. Drop the opposite arm to your bent leg to the side of the ball, and pull the weight up to your armpit, keeping your elbow tucked in as you lift. Keep a slow and controlled tempo, with two sets of 12–15 repetitions.

3+4. Sit ups (abdominals)

Lay on a mat with your feet hip-width apart and your toes pointing forwards. Keep your bum tucked under and your abdominals pulled in. Put your hands behind your head, and make sure your chin is off your chest. Raise your top half from the floor, curling up through the spine, making sure that you don't pull on your neck. Inhale to prepare, and exhale as you move. Aim for two sets of 12–15 repetitions.

5+6. Dorsal raise (lower back)

Lay face down on a mat, with your hands behind your head. Keep your pelvis tucked up, and your feet a little apart. Slowly lift your chest off the floor, and return to the mat. Keep your eyes and head facing down as you move, with a slow and controlled tempo. Aim for two sets of 12–15 repetitions.

exercising in the park

Parks are a favourite of ours and many now have exercise routes, with equipment positioned for you to use as part of an exercise routine.

Exercise routes are only one way of enjoying exercise in a park – you could choose to walk, run, or cycle. The beauty of a park is that it's full of other interesting routes – routes that will act as a guide and make your exercise more interesting. The aim is to get you going and to encourage you to want to do a bit more.

training zone – in the park

1+2. Squats (thighs and bum)

Stand with your head lifted and shoulders back. Keep your abdominals pulled in, your feet hip-width apart, and your toes pointing forwards. Bend slowly, keeping your elbows in line with your knees. Don't let your knees go over your toes, and don't lock your knees whilst you're standing up straight. Keep the tempo slow and controlled, and try two sets of 12–15 repetitions.

3+4. Press ups (chest)

Kneel on the ground with your head up, raising your body from the ground with your hands just over shoulder-width apart, and your elbows slightly bent. Your knees should be under your hips, and your abdominals pulled in. Lower yourself to the ground and raise again at a slow and controlled tempo. Try two sets of 12–15 repetitions.

5+6. Lunges (thighs and bum)

Start by stretching one leg out, so your front knee is in line with your ankle. Your back knee should be under your hip, your back heel up, and your shoulders back. Pull in your lower abdominals as you take your back knee to the floor, and return to the starting position, making sure that your front knee doesn't move forward over your toe. Keep the movement slow and centred, and do two sets of 12–15 repetitions.

staying on track

Firstly – take it easy. If you haven't exercised for years, then your body's unlikely to have the capabilities you remember from your youth; and if you've never really exercised before, don't try too much too soon. The worst that'll happen is you'll get tired and stiff and fed up; the worst thing could be a much more serious injury that puts you out of action for a long time.

But you've started and it's tiring, at first. You're busy and other things seem more pressing (or maybe more of a routine), and you're thinking about packing it in. If that sounds like you, remember that you've already done the hard part in starting. Now consider the following:

Friends and family can be perfect exercise partners. Find someone to walk or jog with you, or accompany you for some or even all of your training sessions. You'll find lots to talk and laugh about – you may find it makes a difference.

Your body will get used to it and want you to do a bit more. This is because your brain is producing endorphins – a sure sign that you are moving in the right direction. We discuss endorphins on page 108.

Remember that by exercising, you'll be burning up calories more quickly than when you started, which is crucial for keeping your waistline trim.

Don't tie yourself down to one form of exercise and let yourself believe it's not for you – if you're getting bored, try new things.

It's OK to treat yourself and have a hard-earned night out. Don't give yourself a hard time about it, just get back into your routine without dwelling on it too much. You could use a weekend night for a treat and then focus on the Monday for getting back into your routine.

Other things that will help

- Make sure you've eaten enough before you exercise, but give your body a chance to digest it properly before you start. If you need to keep your energy levels up while you're exercising, you could try a banana for plenty of slow-release energy.

- Make sure you're drinking water, water, water and more water – try and get to the four pints a day mark. If you're feeling thirsty, you're already dehydrated.

- As you drink more water you'll need less caffeine. You might think it gives you energy, but it's a diuretic so you'll spend hours in the loo, and it'll end up making you dehydrated.

- And finally don't forget that the more you exercise, the more you'll want to. It's always difficult to train your body to adopt a new routine, but suddenly it'll click and you'll experience a massive high.

summary

We weren't born to be idle; don't let our modern, sedentary lives make you feel lazy and out of shape. The sooner you start moving around a bit more – whether it's just a bit each week, or onto moderate fitness you'll soon notice the difference in the way you feel.

There's nothing like going to bed at night physically tired as opposed to mentally drained, or like getting a head start on your day by exercising on the way to work – it really does pick you up for the day ahead.

Energy feeds energy, and the more you do, the more you'll want to do. Start slowly and build it up gradually. Get out there – move about, smell the fresh air, enjoy the scenery and start to sweat.

top ten exercise tips

1 Set small, achievable goals, and give yourself a date to work towards, like a night out, wedding or holiday.

2 Make sure you drink 4–6 pints of water a day. Try and carry a bottle of water with you everywhere you go during the day.

3 Try lots of different types of exercise and find out what you really like.

4 Find a time of day to exercise that suits your schedule: it's no good forcing yourself to exercise before work if you have really early starts, or trying to go after work if you're prone to staying late.

5 Find a training buddy to encourage you, and use your friends and family for support when you're having a down day.

6 Stay away from the scales – it's about how you feel in your clothes, not how much you weigh. Choose certain outfits in your wardrobe and use them as a guide to your progress.

7 Don't give up. We all have bad days, so if things didn't go to plan, get over it and start fresh the next day.

8 Start with little steps. Don't use the lift at work; walk to work; run up and down the stairs or do the gardening. Just start moving around...

9 Reward yourself: there's nothing wrong with a small treat once a week, otherwise you won't find sticking to your plans sustainable.

10 Know what makes you feel good, whether it's a piece of music, a place, a person or an activity. It's about feeling good mentally, as well as physically.

what now?

We're nearly at the end of our 'healthier' tour, but before we finish, we'd like to leave you with these thoughts.

takeaway foods

The facts are frightening and speak for themselves. Walk past takeaways on the way home, eat less of them if you do give in to the urge, be more conscious of what you choose, prepare your own before going out that can be warmed up when you get back home.

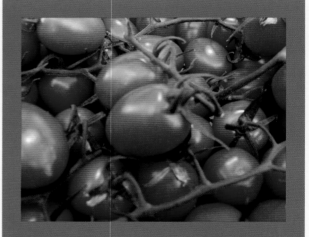

food and cooking

Try to get to your five a day, but if you can't, three a day is fine.

When you're cooking, enjoy it. Become more adventurous, and maybe even take on a few cookery lessons – they're great fun. We'd recommend you treat yourself to a weekend in Nick Nairn's Cookery School in Scotland – it's in a great location, with great staff and great recipes.

nutrition

Water, seeds and routine are all simple steps. Once you are in the groove you may want to seek out the advice of a nutritionist and identify a few more advantages for you and your health.

exercise

You're on your exercise journey and want to stretch yourself more – look up a personal trainer, who'll demonstrate lots of new tips and improvements, work you harder and keep you motivated.

the team

Mike Carney is...
a Liverpool-based graphic designer working with community, arts and health based organisations. Last year he worked with Robbie designing the Can Cook Will Cook book. Mike enjoys a hearty risotto, is partial to the occasional ring donut and would like to do more exercise.

Tony Evans is...
very good with food. He's been the community chef at Fresh for the last four years, and is passionate about introducing new cooking. He works with community groups and schools teaching people with no previous experience how to whip up a healthy, nutritious and tasty meal, and they pick it up in no time...

Robbie Davison is...
passionate about communities having greater control over what happens to them. He's spent 20 years working in the social enterprise world, developing social solutions as a business. He loves music and has a few dislikes too, but says you'll have to ask him about them if you ever meet.

Clare Fox is...
very fit. She's a personal trainer and performance coach with 11 years' experience, and stresses the importance of motivation and target-setting in achieving your goals – in exercise and life in general. She knows you have to feel good on the inside to look and feel good on the outside, and is a firm believer in never giving up.

Lucy Parkes...
loves engaging school pupils through creative
learning. She is involved in a range of projects
to improve learning in schools and has been
integral to the success of the Can Cook Will Cook
School Sessions.

Helen Turner is...
a devoted water drinker. She's a nutritional
therapist, and owner of Helen Turner Nutrition,
a consultancy for everything natural nutrition.
She covers a range of services including one to
one consultations, community projects, corporate
well being, events, media, food, cooking and
education, and is an advocate of the restorative
power of flax.

Fiona Shaw is...
the one who spends most of her time sitting at a
computer. She's a director of Capsica, Healthier's
publishers, but wishes she worked outside. She's
working on a range of non-fiction books, and
documenting Liverpool's year as European Capital
of Culture in photos. She loves music and footie,
and could probably do with a bit more running
around herself.

Alexandra Wolkowicz is...
a Polish German photographer now resident in
Liverpool. Her work extends from portraiture to
music, art and documentary photography, often
engaging with local communities. She's into yoga
and swimming, enjoys trying new food and can't
resist a free buffet.

finally...

Healthier is a whistle-stop tour of ideas we hope will make you feel healthier and happier. We don't want to force you to change your lives, give up your favourite things, or follow a routine so punishing and puritanical it lasts just for a few days. Our aim with Healthier was to approach the idea of health in a more holistic way; healthier food, a bit more exercise, a greater understanding of what we're putting into our bodies, and to build on what you already know. There are some cracking ideas suggested in each section, and they have been compiled by practitioners who are both devoted to the career disciplines and who spend their working lives wanting to share their experience and techniques.

For us, it was important not to treat the sections in isolation, we've tried to do something different, and take a look at the complete package. There's no 'one-size-fits-all' solution, we've tried to give you choices. A bit less of one thing, a bit more of another, and in some ways we are just scratching the surface. You may well now want to look a little or lot deeper into some things – now you have had read what we have had to say.

We hope in your eyes, we have achieved what we set out to do – and after you have tried and tested our suggestions, you are that much healthier for it. Now that would be job done.

acknowledgments

Robbie would like to thank...

Tony: for the hard work and skill to pull all of the recipes together and make the Can Cook sessions what they are – you are a natural trainer.

Lucy: For your commitment, judgement and support for both this project and your co-ordination of the School Sessions.

Mike: Yet another great piece of design – it was harder this time around, but sometimes it takes a while – the results are worth it – cheers mate.

Fiona: The organiser, the counsellor, the timekeeper, the mediator – a really big thank you for keeping it all together.

Alex: The pictures capture the whole project and bring it all to life – thanks also for letting us invade your place.

Clare: Thanks for letting us in on some of your secrets – the section is just right – enjoyed it.

Helen: It all makes sense; no coffee, lots of water and the odd enema – I'm hooked.

Dave and Rachel: The facts set the scene to the book – takeaways are a bit scarier now. Thank you to you both.

Paddy and Tom: Great staff, food, bistro, atmosphere – you deserve your success.

Graham and Ann: You have created a real trip to the country – thanks for letting us look around. Alex loved the donkey and chasing the chicken.

Vicky: Writer of the serotonin and endorphins sections – for providing us with the science to explain how we were feeling and why. It pulls it all together.

The internet is a great source of information and inspiration. We like what people like Michael Pollan have to say about all things foodie – look out for his book 'In Defence of Food'.

Bibliography:
'Carbohydrate ingestion, blood glucose and mood';
David Benton, Neuroscience & Biobehavioural Reviews;
002, 26(3) 293-308

The supporters:
Susan: for daring to make the centre different.
Julie Curren: what can I say – thanks again.
Irene Mills: For believing in it all and always supporting us.

For your assistance:
Liverpool City Council Trading Standards and **Liverpool John Moores University** for allowing access to their work on takeaway food.
Gill Faure of David Lloyd Speke – for letting us in to photograph the exercise section.

Everyday Cooking for Everyday People

about can cook will cook

Almost every day we hear that we're becoming more unhealthy. Obesity is a national concern and it seems that the effects are touching almost every family at some level. Our day job is working with children and families and our chef and his team prepare food for lots of children and parents who visit our centres. Not everything we do is the healthiest – it just isn't practical – but everything we do is thought about to make it that bit healthier. We realised long ago that we all have different tastes, different expectations and are full of different experiences, so to try and come up with a one size fits all healthy eating plan is unreasonable.

Being realistic is what drives what we do. Our cafés continue to improve their menus and as a consequence, our customers are always improving their diets in a small way. They're little steps, but they matter.

This year we've started to work with new schools and groups on new initiatives, all of which have cookery and food as their inspiration. As you read this, hundreds of people – young and old – have been trained. It's what we love to do and it's through the books that we're able to share the benefits of this training with a much wider audience. We would love to run a Can Cook programme in every town and every city and maybe sometime in the future this will happen. Until then, this book is the next best thing. Thanks for reading.

The Can Cook Will Cook programme is one aspect of the enterprise of a charity based in Liverpool, which is all about improving the lives of children and families. Every time you purchase a book, the proceeds go towards supporting this work. You can find out all about it at www.cancookwillcook.org.uk

Can Cook Will Cook is a project of Five Children and Families Trust. Charity no 1112796

index